Coinage of the Americas Conference

Proceedings No. 9

Proceedings
of the
Coinage of the Americas Conference

America's Silver Dollars

EDITED BY

John M. Kleeberg

Coinage of the Americas Conference
at The American Numismatic Society, New York

October 30, 1993

Illustrations for each article have been supplied by the authors, supplemented by photographs of ANS specimens where appropriate.

The American Numismatic Society
Broadway at 155th Street
New York, NY 10032
212/234-3130

Printed in the United States of America

Contents

Preface

The United States Silver Dollar provided the subject for the ninth annual Coinage of the Americas Conference sponsored by the American Numismatic Society. Since its inception, this program has enjoyed the enthusiastic support of the Society's governing Council as a forum for the dissemination of emerging research in the coinage and currency of North and South America.

The purpose of these conferences is to facilitate the exchange of information. Toward this end, experts in the field are invited to present papers, collectors are invited to exhibit, and notice of the conference is circulated widely to encourage attendance by all interested in the topic. The Society also mounts an exhibition from its holdings and invites registrants to come to know the Society's collections and library better during the days of the conference.

A special exhibit on the history of the silver dollar was put together by Modern Curator John M. Kleeberg and Registrar Katharina Eldada. The exhibit showed the silver dollar from the standing archduke thaler of Archduke Sigismund of the Tirol to the present day, including silver crowns struck by the United States Mint for other countries. The United States Mint also participated, exhibiting their modern commemorative issues of silver dollars.

Contributors

The Society is grateful to the following contributors who helped make the 1993 Coinage of the Americas Conference possible:

Leslie A. Elam   R. Henry Norweb, Jr.
Dr. Jay M. Galst   Donald G. Partrick
Joseph R. Lasser   Richard J. Reinhardt
Allen F. Lovejoy   P. Scott Rubin
A. George Mallis   Edward J. Rudnicki
Emmett McDonald

The American Numismatic Association
The David and Sharon R. Ganz Endowment, ANA
The United States Mint

Introduction

In the first decades of the sixteenth century, the Counts of Šlik, lords of the fabulously rich mine in St. Joachim's valley in the Ore Mountains on the Saxo-Bohemian border, began to mint a new large size silver coin. It was soon referred to as "the coin from St. Joachim's valley," or the Joachimsthaler - abbreviated to thaler, which later would be anglicized to dollar. When the United States won its independence in 1783, the very successful Mexican version of the dollar, the *real de a ocho*, was the most common coin in circulation in the colonies. It was natural to choose it as the basis of the monetary system of the colonies.

Unfortunately, if the Counts of Šlik and the mintmasters of Mexico met with success, the same cannot be said of the United States. The attempts by the United States to produce a dollar coin in silver (and later, in copper-nickel) have repeatedly met with failure. With a role in several financial panics (1857 and 1893/5), and at least seven illicit special productions (1804 dollars, 1866 no motto dollars, 1884 and 1885 trade dollars, 1921 proofs, 1964 dollars), the checkered history of the silver dollar clearly has much interest for specialists in the United States series. It was for this reason that the COAC committee chose U.S. silver dollars as the theme for the 1993 Coinage of the Americas Conference.

The first attempts to mint dollars met with delays because the minters could not post the surety bond required. After the amount of the bond was reduced in 1794, the minting of precious metal coins began. The new coins were not a success. Most silver bullion in the early United States was in the form of Mexican eight reales, which remained a legal tender until 1857. There was no incentive for merchants to bring Mexican dollars to the mint to be recoined into United States dollars; not only would they have to pay the cost of the minting, but they would also lose interest on their money while they waited for it to be coined into dollars. One of the few reasons for recoining silver at the mint was brought out by Robert

D. Leonard, Jr., when he delivered the Stack Memorial Lecture in April 1994 at the American Numismatic Society: to recoin cut silver coins into a more acceptable form.

When silver was recoined into dollars, it was rapidly exported. Three early U.S. dollars are known with private Scottish mercantile countermarks. (They are discussed in more detail in Robert Stark's and my contributions below.) But most U.S. dollars did not stop their journey in Britain. The dollars would be bought up by the East India Company, which would then send them onward to China, where they were used to buy tea. Only the development of the opium trade gradually brought some relief from the relentless silver drain to China. Many early date dollars probably ended up by being melted and cast as sycee ingots.

President Thomas Jefferson sought to cut off this silver drain. Just as he sought to isolate the country from the problems of Europe with his quixotic embargo, so he sought to cut down on the export of silver by ending the mintage of the classic trade coins: the dollar and the eagle. Henceforth, the half dollar would be the workhorse coin for bank transactions. The first attempt at an U.S. silver dollar had ended in failure.

Although the mint made no silver dollars dated 1804, it continued to coin in that year using 1803 dated dies. In 1838, one of the most famous non-coin coins was created by Mint employees: the 1804 dollar. This artificial rarity proved extremely useful for swapping for rare pieces lacking from the Mint's collection and for supplementing the income of Mint officials.

In the 1830s, a new attempt was made at coining silver dollars. Christian Gobrecht produced one of the most attractive silver dollar designs—the flying eagle dollars. Small amounts were minted in 1836–39. From 1840, the Mint began to strike more dollars, but they never circulated extensively, because the rise in gold production made silver more valuable compared to gold. The silver dollars disappeared into hoards. In 1857, the legal tender status of Mexican dollars was revoked. Unfortunately, this was during a silver shortage. Austria, under the brilliant finance minister Freiherr von Bruck, was hoarding silver so it could redeem its paper currency. In India, the outbreak of the Mutiny led to more demands on the silver market. The Taiping rebellion in China was a further drain. By revoking the legal tender status of Mexican dollars, yet another strain was put on the silver market when it could ill afford it. The market would have to rely on gold for specie. On August 24, 1857, the Ohio Life and Trust Company collapsed. On September 12, 1857, the SS *Central America* was wrecked off Cape Hatteras. The panic was there, and nothing could stop it. It gripped the commercial centers of North America, passed on to Northern Europe, especially Hamburg and Scandinavia, and even affected merchants in Rio de Janeiro, Montevideo and Buenos Aires, Valparaiso and Guayaquil, and far-off Batavia. Most of the major mercantile houses of Hamburg (which relied on the silver standard) collapsed. Only gold standard Bremen remained immune.[1]

During the Civil War, silver was hoarded, along with all other hard currency. In 1873, the coinage of silver dollars was quietly ended, and replaced by the trade dollar; but the collapse of silver prices led trade dollars to flood into the United States. In 1878, the Mint ceased to make them for circulation. Instead, the United States embarked upon the monumental folly of the Morgan dollar and the Sherman silver act, which compelled the treasury to buy 187.5 tons of silver a month. As this silver poured into the treasury, the public, nervous about the country's commitment to the gold standard, drained the Treasury of gold. The result was the panic of 1893. The crises of the mid-1890s made it clear that this expensive subsidy to the mining interest could not continue. The issue was put clearly before the public in the election of 1896, and the public rejected the utopian plans of Bryan and went with McKinley and the gold standard. By 1904, the Treasury had used up its stock of silver, and the minting of Morgan dollars came to an end.

In 1921, coinage resumed to replace the dollars melted under the Pittman act. Clandestine proofs were also made. In 1921, a new design, the Peace dollar, replaced the Morgan dollar. Mintage of the Peace dollar ended in 1928, but was resumed in 1934 and 1935 to subsidize Western mineowners. In 1964, the Mint again coined silver dollars, but was so embarrassed by the publicity that it recalled and claims to have melted all of them.

The most recent attempt to introduce a dollar coin in the United States—the Susan B. Anthony dollar—again met with failure. The government tried to force the Susan B. Anthony coins into circulation by paying armed forces personnel in Germany only in $2 bills and Susan B. Anthony dollars. In December 1980, however, the Deutsche Bank declared that it would henceforth exchange Susan B. Anthony dollars at the rate of only one Deutsche Mark per dollar, at time when paper dollars were trading at 1.75 Deutsche Marks per dollar. This meant that armed forces personnel had undergone a major pay-cut. The U.S. Mint went toe-to-toe with the Deutsche Bank; the outcome was never seriously in doubt. In January 1981, the Treasury had to abandon this experiment, and since then the Susan B. Anthony coins have gathered dust in Treasury vaults, carried on the books at their dollar value rather than their insignificant melt value. The Treasury refuses to take the loss, hoping it will be able to get rid of them somehow.[2]

Some of this history is covered in more detail in the following pages, including much that is new. Eric P. Newman resolves one of the most controversial topics, the origin of the dollar sign. His article is particularly welcome, because many false explanations have become part of popular culture. Jules Reiver, who has inspired much research in the history of the early mint, gives a personal overview of the bust dollars. Kenneth Bressett details one of the most exciting new discoveries in the bust dollar series: the silver plug in the dollars of 1795. Professor Robert Stark discusses the various countermarks on early U.S. silver dollars.

At one coin club I attended, a member brought in a Morgan dollar with a counterstamp which turned out to be a modern fantasy, although a rather interesting piece nonetheless. One of the fellow members said, "Now you have to VAM it." "Vam it?" "Determine the die variety from the work of Van Allen and Mallis." The "M" in this remarkable verb, Lieutenant-Colonel A. George Mallis, surveys the development of the designs of the 1878 Morgan dollar. Finally, I outline the problem of why the silver dollar was never able to make its way in international trade.

Two appendices close the volume. Eric P. Newman gives a useful review of what we know about the 1804 dollar. I provide an account of two 1883-CC Morgan dollar dies which are in the collection of the American Numismatic Society.

John M. Kleeberg
Conference Chairman

---

[1]   Max Wirth, *Geschichte der Handelskrisen* (Vienna, 1890), pp. 245-418.

[2]   Walter Breen, *Walter Breen's Complete Encyclopedia of U.S. and Colonial Coins* (New York, 1988), p. 472.

The Dollar $ign
Its Written and Printed Origins

Eric P. Newman

**Coinage of the Americas Conference
at the American Numismatic Society, New York**

October 30, 1993

The written English language is and has been read from left to right just as have other European languages. Hebrew, Arabic and some other Asian languages are and have customarily been read from right to left. An exception in the English language is the $ sign as accompanied by one or more numerals to its right. For example, in reading $6 the number is read first and the monetary symbol thereafter, so that such an amount is read from right to left instead of from left to right. This order of reading is and has for many centuries been used with respect to the symbol £ for the English monetary pound. Other countries have also followed such a practice of reading their own monetary symbols after the numerals even though numerals are placed to the right of their symbols. This practice is complicated theoretically in left to right reading when more than one numeral is used in a number because such a number is first read from left to right before the monetary symbol on the left of the numerals is added. The human mind easily adjusts to these conditions without the eyes changing direction.[1]

The practice of writing in a manner to cause this exception developed as a matter of convenience and practicality in written money records and in calculations as will be more obvious from examples included in this study.

The uncertainty as to the origin of the conventional $ sign was pointed out in the fourth edition (1859) of *Webster's Unabridged Dictionary.* Curiosity continued to develop and in 1865 an instructional monetary treatise by Wilber and Eastman was published as a promotion for the successful Eastman Commercial College and pointed out the then existing controversy.[2] For more than a century thereafter theories and explanations abounded.

The theories included:

1. The letters U.S. for United States or Uncle Sam were combined in ligature and the bottom loop to the U abandoned.

2. The letters ps or Ps as the Spanish abbreviation of pesos were superimposed on one another and the top loop of the p or P abandoned.

3. The first and last letters of the Spanish word "fuertes" (meaning hard money or specie coin) were combined in ligature.

4. The Spanish symbol for the 8 reales coin or piece of 8 was written as 8 or |8| or 8-8 or 8||8 or p8 and combined in ligature.

5. The Straits of Gibraltar, known as the Pillars of Hercules, were represented by two upright columns in various forms on Spanish and Spanish American coinage with a ribbon or scroll draped across the uprights and these were combined in ligature.

6.   The two upright columns representing the Pillars of Hercules on Spanish and Spanish American coinage were combined in ligature with an S for the English spelling of Spain or Spanish.

7.   The denomination of 2½ asses (a sestertius) on some Roman Republican coinage, written IIS (textually 1-1 S), was combined in ligature.

8.   The religious motto "In Hoc Signo" was often abbreviated I H S and combined in ligature, the $ sign being a reworking of it.

9.   In Spanish American coinage from the Columbian Mint at San Luis Potosi the mint mark of SLP in ligature was reworked and adapted.

10.   The Portuguese symbol for cifrao (phonetically cifron) meaning thousand was copied.

11.   The first and last letters of the Portuguese word Milhores (thousands) were combined in ligature.

12.   The symbol £ for pound sterling was adapted and changed into an S for Spanish superimposed with a vertical line or lines instead of a horizontal line or lines as in the £ symbol.

13.   The letters Ds or DS as an abbreviation for dollars were superimposed on one another and reworked.

14.   A variety of Chinese hollow handle spade bronze coinage from about 350 B.C. contains a mirror image $ sign which is read Mi chin. Henry Ramsden humorously suggested it as a source.

The present summary of a century of prior historical research on the $ sign, supplemented with additional findings and thoughts may therefore be welcome.

The Need for a Symbol

The Spanish and Spanish American silver coins known as pieces of 8 reals (reales) were customarily referred to in commercial transactions in eighteenth century America, when the English language was used, as the dollar, the Spanish dollar, the Spanish milled dollar, the Spanish American dollar, the Peru dollar, the Mexican dollar, the silver dollar, the cross dollar, the pillar dollar, the bust dollar, etc. For Spanish speaking people such coins were called the peso or peso duro. For French speaking people those coins were referred to as the piastre, a term of Italian origin. Technically there were some design, weight and fineness variations in the coins from time to time but the varied expressions describing them were internationally understood by the commercial world and by the American public.

Money calculations are usually performed in one's native language, whether written, spoken, or only mental. An abbreviation or symbol for such a monetary unit simplifies the writing of the unit for everyone regardless of language, just as is true as to the written use of numbers or numerals. To have a common symbol for a monetary unit which everyone might use in writing was a great advantage in bookkeeping, communication and commercial transactions regardless of the language a person used to refer to that monetary unit. Thus it would be a convenience for British colonists in America doing business in Spanish, French or English speaking regions to have a practical symbol for the primary coin used in payments and trading transactions. The Spanish were using ps, pS, Ps and PS as abbreviations for pesos, customarily written with flourishes and rubrica and often involving more than one horizontal level of writing. These abbreviations consisted of two letters of the alphabet and were written in script or capitals in both upper and lower case. To use any form of ps as a symbol for the English word dollar was somewhat confusing and cumbersome. Calculations needed a monetary symbol like the British £ (libra) which was entirely distinctive and did not have to be repeated when extensively used. A symbol had to avoid interference with addition, subtraction, multiplication and division as well as not blocking columnization or extension. It had to be different from all numerals and lettering and be able to be placed close to them. The abbreviation in English of d or D for dollar had been used occasionally but was not distinctive because it could be confused with d, the common abbreviation for English pence (denarius) or American money of account pence. Combinations like dl, ds, dls, dol, dols, dolls and dollrs were used but consisted of lettering and were not brief enough. Even Thomas Jefferson who enjoyed adopting new concepts wrote D with a horizontal line through it during his lifetime as his choice for a distinct symbol for dollar, obviously having been influenced by the horizontal line or lines used in the British monetary symbol £. Neither he nor his contemporaries seem to have commented upon the use of the $ sign even though some of them used it.

In the eastern portion of the English Colonies in North America prior to the American Revolution, there was no critical need to have a practical symbol to refer to the dollar because it was not a primary or official monetary unit except to some extent in Maryland beginning in 1767. Even though the dollar was a commonly used expression for a Spanish or Spanish American peso as a trade coin and as a standard of exchange value it was not the basic unit for American prices and bookkeeping. The decimal system as to amounts less than one dollar was not then used. During the American Revolution the

Continental Congress and the independent states spread the use of the dollar as a bookkeeping unit by issuing paper money in dollar denominations to try to create economic uniformity and stability. In 1782, after the end of military action, Gouverneur Morris, through Robert Morris, recommended a dollar of 1440 mills as a basis for money of account for all states with a new 1000 mill Federal coin of proportionately lower value as the largest silver coin.[3] Thomas Jefferson and others felt this to be impractical. The United States on July 6, 1785, adopted the dollar both as a monetary standard and as the largest silver coin, the cent becoming the dollar's basic decimal subdivision. Thus the broader need to use a distinctive symbol for the dollar became even more essential because of the official federal abandonment of all money of account systems in coinage plans. Such a symbol, the $ sign, was already developed and in use by English speaking merchants along the northern coast of the Gulf of Mexico but minimally elsewhere in the United States. Since habits of people in writing and bookkeeping are particularly slow to change, the acceptance and use of the $ sign had a gradual metamorphosis in the United States thereafter.

The $ Sign Discoveries by Cajori

Florian Cajori (1858-1930), a professor of mathematics, physics and engineering who taught at Tulane University, The Colorado College and the University of California (Berkeley), is responsible for initiating and vigorously continuing a factual study of the history of the $ sign. Prior to his research the many theories which abounded had no probative support. In a 1912 article, Cajori published an assembly of peso or dollar marks from the sixteenth through the eighteenth centuries from various parts of the world (fig. 1).[4] He showed in a chart that the abbreviation for the plural of pesos was written in various ways and that the s in the abbreviation ps was often at a level above the p. He also pointed out that the handwriting of the abbreviation ps often was done in one stroke of the pen and that a capital P was not customary. He noticed that in Mexico until after independence from Spain in 1821 the Mexicans continued to use the abbreviation ps for pesos as they had done in the eighteenth century.

He concluded that the $ sign was developed about 1775 in North America by English speaking Americans who were in business contact with Spanish speaking Americans and that the earliest known written use of the $ sign was by Oliver Pollock of New Orleans in an August 29, 1778 letter to George Rogers Clark. He also stated that the first printed use of the $ sign was in Chauncey Lee's

Eric P. Newman

Place of MS.	Date of MS.			Date of MS.	Place of MS.
Spain	abt. 1500			1598 .	Mexico City
Mexico (?)	1601			1633	San Felipe de puerto
Mexico	1644			1649	Mexico City
Manila	1672			1696	Mexico
Mexico	1718			1746	Mexico City
Chietla (Mexico)	1748			1766	Manila
Mexico	1768			1769	?
New Orleans	1778			(1778) 1783	New Orleans
				1786	New Orleans
Mexico City	1781			1787	Mexico City
On the Mississippi	1787				
Philadelphia	1792			1793	" Nouvelle Madrid " (N. O.)
" Nouvelle Madrid " (N. O.)	1794			1794	" Nouvelle Madrid " (N. O.)
" Nouvelle Madrid " (N. O.)	1794			1794	" Nouvelle Madrid " (N. O.)
New Orleans	1796			1796	Philadelphia (?)
New Orleans	1796			1799	Louisville (?)

1

American Accomptant published in 1797.[5]

Cajori's article attracted customary challenges, corrections and new data which he was prompt to report.[6] Cajori detailed data provided by August H. Fiske from the diary of Ezra L'Hommedieu, an attorney of Southhold, New York, who was a deputy from Suffolk County to the Provincial Assembly of New York (after July 9, 1776, Convention of Representatives of the State of New York) and attended meetings at Poughkeepsie, White Plains, and Fishkill from June 10 to December 5, 1776.

L'Hommedieu's entries include items in pounds and shillings (New York money of account rather than sterling) and dollars. Dollar amounts are spelled out until August 21, 1776, when there appears "Treasurer to advance Captain Wismer $580 for bounty." On August 24, 1776, there is a reversion to "Hugh Doyle is to receive 8 dollars." Then on August 28, 1776, "the treasurer is to advance $10 for removing military stores from New York" is entered. Then follow many uses of the $ sign. Up to October 31, 1776, a single stroke crosses the S while thereafter two strokes are used. These entries moved the earliest use of the $ sign to 1776 and geographically distant from Spanish speaking areas (fig. 2).

Aug. 21	Aug. 28	Oct. 2	Oct. 31

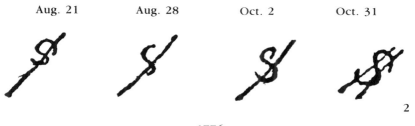

2

1776

In a 1925 article, Cajori corrects himself about the first $ sign in print being in Chauncey Lee's 1797 publication.[7] He emphasizes the differences in Lee's symbols from the conventional version already in use before 1797 and assumes that Lee knew what was then in use. Cajori is thus the first to emphasize that Lee's symbols are unrelated to the conventional $ sign, but he does not consider the probability that Lee could have been entirely unfamiliar with the conventional $ sign. Lee's publication will be detailed subsequently herein.

In 1929, Cajori again updated his research,[8] presenting a slave sale document in Spanish from Puerto Rico, dated April 1, 1778, in which the amount of 478 pesos, 5 reales, 16 maravedis is writ-

ten as "quatrociemos sesenta y ocho ps $ cinco rrs y diez & siete
mrv" (fig. 3).

*un Negro Mulecon, y una Negra Muleco-
na, en precio de quatrocientos sesenta y
ocho p. $ cinco rrs y diez y riete mrv; los
que ha rezivido el Factor D.n Pedro de
Laurea.*   3

This item shows the $ sign being used as a repetition of ps for
plural purposes and follows it with a double r for pluralizing the
abbreviation for reales. Cajori repeats his prior findings and recon-
firms them. When Florian Cajori died in 1930 he had passed forward a heritage of accurate information on the $ sign which others
might build upon.

The John Fitzpatrick Letterbooks

By the secret Treaty of Fontainebleau on November 3, 1762 (the
formal Treaty of Paris was signed February 10, 1763), the Louisiana
Territory on the west side of the Mississippi River and the area surrounding New Orleans on the east side was transferred from France
to Spain, while the balance of the French territory on the east side
of the Mississippi River was added to the English colonies in America.
The Spanish also yielded East and West Florida to the English. The
English obtained non-exclusive navigation rights on the entire
Mississippi River. The news of the Treaty did not reach New Orleans
until September 1764. Naturally the French then lost interest in the
administration of the Louisiana Territory area and left it to the
Spanish to redeem the outstanding French paper money obligations
there. American colonial traders, many from the Atlantic seaboard,
promptly moved to New Orleans in the new Spanish Territory and
to Florida Gulf of Mexico ports in the new English territory to take
advantage of the slack in commercial activity due to the changes
in ownership. A few established themselves upstream on the rivers
on which furs were shipped. The Spanish were slow to take over
administration of the Louisiana Territory and in 1766 sent Antoine
de Ulloa to New Orleans as Governor without adequate support or
supplies. He retained many French officials and was ejected in the

local revolt of 1768. In August 1769, however, Spain sent in Alejandro O'Reilly as Governor with adequate military and economic backing to enforce Spanish control.

Under the prior French administration of the Louisiana Territory the livre was used as the basic unit of money of account in commerce. The livre and its fractions were not represented by any French specie coin but by deerskin and other skins as commodities and by balances on account books of merchants and traders. There was also paper money consisting of card money, treasury notes, promissory notes, certificates of credit and bons. In view of intermittent French colonial inflation and fluctuations in the value of skins there were customary negotiated conversion rates of the livre into the piastre (the dollar or peso).

By 1769 the English traders who had moved into the Gulf areas were dominating the exports and imports, primarily using the peso in the Louisiana Territory area as the unit of monetary value in place of the French livre. Thus the livre as a money of account began a lingering phase-out in the Mississippi Valley and the peso solidified itself there both as a specie coin and as the monetary unit for bookkeeping purposes. West Florida being formerly Spanish territory routinely continued its peso usage. The English colonies on the North American Atlantic coast were primarily using and continued to use pounds, shillings and pence as their several moneys of account with various exchange value ratios to the peso or Spanish dollar. During the American Revolution, the Continental Currency of the United Colonies (United States after July 1776) and the paper money of some of the independent American States selected the ''Spanish dollar'' as their monetary unit for paper money and to some extent their money of account practices even though there were few Spanish silver dollars in circulation.

Governor O'Reilly recognized the domination of trade and the smuggling practices of the English colonists operating their trading establishments in New Orleans and promptly ordered them to leave the Spanish area on September 2, 1769. Many of them moved to Mobile, Pensacola and inland locations in British owned West Florida and continued their trade. This greatly increased the use of a special route to transport merchandise up and down most of the Mississippi River without passing by New Orleans where inspection and fees were imposed by the Spanish. There was a way to leave the Mississippi River at Bayou Manchac (then also known as the Iberville River) 8 miles south of Baton Rouge, continue eastwardly along Bayou Manchac to the Amite River, and then proceed southerly through Lake Maurepas and Lake Ponchartrain into the Gulf of Mexico. This route was a bypass from all of the Mississippi River Valley slightly north of New Orleans to the Gulf of Mexico, the bypass being entirely under British jurisdiction at that time.

One of the expelled English colonists was John Fitzpatrick. He was born in Waterford, Ireland in 1737. He served three and a half years as an English colonial ranger under Robert Rogers during the French and Indian War. In 1762 he was a trader in the Illinois area working for Oakes & Goddard. He was captured by native Americans but escaped. In 1764 he visited Mobile in West Florida, returning to Illinois in 1765. When he moved to New Orleans is not certain but he was well established there by 1768. When he was ordered to leave in 1769, he tried to liquidate his assets and pay his debts, but left for Mobile on September 21, 1769, before that could be accomplished. He arranged to open a store on high ground at Manchac (Fort Bute) at the juncture of Bayou Manchac and the Mississippi River and moved there by February 15, 1770. His friend Isaac Monsanto who was also expelled from New Orleans already had opened a store in Manchac. Fitzpatrick lived in Manchac during the Revolutionary War and the subsequent Spanish occupation until his death on March 20, 1791. His wife survived until 1797 and all their assets were sold to pay debts—all except an unsalable chest of papers and records containing his business letterbooks which have turned out to be the major resource for the history of the $ sign.

There are almost 1,000 commercial letters copied by Fitzpatrick and his clerks into the letterbooks. They are written at New Orleans from June 13, 1768 through September 21, 1769, at Mobile from November 7, 1769 through December 12, 1769, and at Manchac from February 15, 1770 through May 21, 1790. Most of the letters are to merchants in Pensacola, Mobile, New Orleans and Natchez. Some are to traders in towns along the Mississippi River and its tributaries. They are replete with prices, accounts due, accounts receivable, exchange matters, note obligations, expenses, calculations and other money matters. They are almost all in English (a few in French), full of spelling and grammatical errors, colloquial expressions and with Spanish, English, French and American monetary abbreviations and symbols galore. Florian Cajori was unaware of the existence of the letterbooks.

In 1978 Margaret Fisher Dalrymple completed a study of the Fitzpatrick letterbooks and the text of each letter was published by the Louisiana State University Press along with her historical introduction, glossary, etc.[9] Given that the condition of the letterbooks was mediocre, her ability to decipher crudely penned backwoods English was outstanding. She included symbols and abbreviations as written, unveiling the amazing facility of her hard working merchant pauper to demonstrate the convenience and practicality of the $ sign and his part in developing it as early as June 30, 1768 (fig. 4).

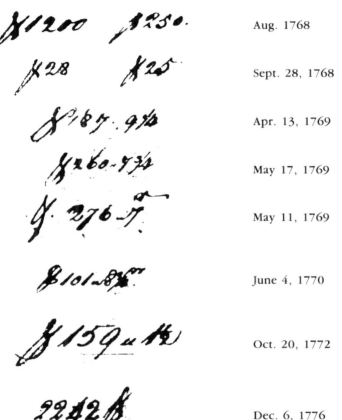

	Aug. 1768
	Sept. 28, 1768
	Apr. 13, 1769
	May 17, 1769
	May 11, 1769
	June 4, 1770
	Oct. 20, 1772
	Dec. 6, 1776 4

The use of the $ sign in early manuscript communications is complicated by the fact that often the only known written text is not necessarily written by the signer of the letter or by the preparer of a retained copy in a letterbook or otherwise. The scribe or secretary sometimes wrote the letter and it was then signed by the principal. On other occasions the principal wrote and signed the entire letter and the scribe or secretary prepared necessary duplicates which were sent in case of loss of the original or which were for retention or both. It seems reasonable to presume that duplicates or copies prepared by scribes customarily repeated the symbols as originally written because any changes might be considered inaccurate and subject to criticism. The important fact is that both sender and receiver of a communication understood the symbols which were used. The $ sign would not have been used by the sender if the receiver would not have fully understood it. As its convenience was recognized it was used more and more by senders and spread to others who at first were reluctant to use it.

In the Fitzpatrick letterbooks most of the copies of the letters are in Fitzpatrick's own hand, an indication that he also wrote those original letters.

From the beginning of the letterbooks in 1768, Fitzpatrick uses a special symbol for dollars which is not "pS". It is used over 1,000 times in his letterbooks. It is created with one continuous stroke going downward obliquely to the left, then continuing upwardly for an equal distance near the left side of the downstroke and finally obliquely downward to the right in a reversing curve across the other two parts of the symbol. The lower portions of p in pS are evident in the first downward and upward portions of the stroke. The final part of the stroke is an S curve. There is no trace of the top loop of the p. The S curve is superimposed on the two other portions of the stroke.

There has been nothing located prior to 1776 to compare with these symbols. They could not have been related to U S because there was no United States at that time. The joinder at the bottom of the first two parts of the symbol dismisses any relationship to the parallel Pillars of Hercules on the coinage. All uses by Fitzpatrick of his special symbol were to represent the dollar. The convenience and clarity of the form of this symbol is obvious. The fact that the top loop of the p is omitted might not by itself be considered by some as sufficient to make the Fitzpatrick symbol distinctive, but the superimposition of the S over the two lower portions of the p is the major additional change of form. Fitzpatrick never had to explain the meaning of his symbols to anyone in his correspondence and his addressees clearly understood what he was using. Whether he learned from others the symbol he used or vice versa does not detract from his own extensive use of it.

Symbols and abbreviations for dollars and pesos are often used interchangeably in the letterbooks with a lack of uniformity in placement relative to the numerals indicating the amount. In a Fitzpatrick letter written July 17, 1769, from New Orleans to a merchant at Mobile "71½ Ds," "$164.6½," and "Ds 401:4" are all written in the first paragraph. In another letter to Pensacola on the same date the abbreviation "ps" has two different meanings when sail cloth "was charged 5 ps per yard which is $ 15 Ds per ps," with "ps" first used meaning dollars and then meaning piece. The plural of pieces is sometimes abbreviated in the letterbooks as "pss" to distinguish it from money.

On May 9, 1771, a letter from Manchac to Pensacola again has different symbols with the same meaning in the same sentence when Fitzpatrick writes "Amounts to ps 337.2r of which there is for you $137.2r and the other $200 for Mr. John Stephensons Accot." On November 9, 1771, a Fitzpatrick letter from Manchac to Mobile includes "$24 Ds."

In a July 19, 1772 Fitzpatrick letter, a price was described as "some at 8½ $ and Others at 9 Dollers." In another letter dated October 7, 1773, an amount is written as "$ 5 Dollers," showing the same monetary standard on each side of the numerals, but in different form. In a May 17, 1769 Fitzpatrick letter written from New Orleans to a Pensacola merchant, it is stated that "It will be 1½ Dollar for the Corn and Barrel here if shipped in this place, and if obliged to send it to the Bayoux will stand you in $1 - 6. Exclusive of freight." On October 20, 1772, "$159.1½" and "Ds 159.6½r" are both used referring to the same group of merchandise.

While the amount of reals is often indicated only with punctuation following dollar amounts, sometimes both dollars and reals are specifically designated with variations such as a redundance in February 1771, using "$ 128.4½rs In hard Dollers" and a partial use of symbols in "383 Dollers 1½rs" on July 19, 1772.

In addition to what is heretofore shown, the $ sign occasionally follows an amount in the manner spoken, such as "35 $" on September 28, 1768, "8½ $" on July 19, 1772, "2242 $" on December 6, 1776, and "2 $" and "1 $" on July 8, 1777.

Fitzpatrick's facility in using seven different money symbols and abbreviations is demonstrated in a November 21, 1776 letter from Manchac to Baton Rouge in which he calculated the exchange value of 6 pounds, 5 shillings, 4 pence in English Sterling into dollars and reals at the rate of 4 shillings, 8 pence Sterling per dollar. It may also be observed how similar his abbreviation for "per" is to the common use of "ps" as a symbol for "pesos" (fig. 5).

Those whose native language was Spanish had remained satisfied in the eighteenth century with the abbreviation ps or pS for peso but for convenience in foreign trade sometimes used the $ sign as well. Just as in the 1778 Puerto Rican slave sale document previously illustrated, there is a May 4, 1778 letter written by a scribe from Spanish Governor Estevan Miro at New Orleans to Thomas McKean

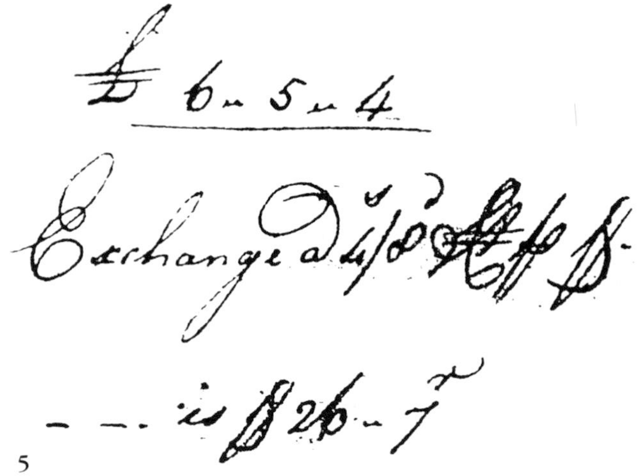

£ 6..5(s) ..(d)

Exchange at
4s8d St pr $

is $26..7r

5

in Philadelphia with an amount written in numerals followed by
a repetition of the same double symbol. It is "30355 pS $" and has
the capital S in pS in script rather than in Roman style (fig. 6).

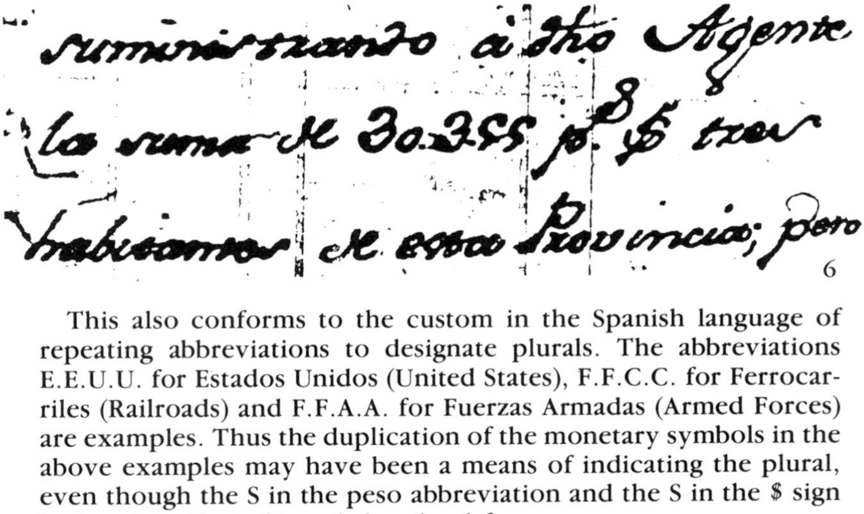

6

This also conforms to the custom in the Spanish language of
repeating abbreviations to designate plurals. The abbreviations
E.E.U.U. for Estados Unidos (United States), F.F.C.C. for Ferrocar-
riles (Railroads) and F.F.A.A. for Fuerzas Armadas (Armed Forces)
are examples. Thus the duplication of the monetary symbols in the
above examples may have been a means of indicating the plural,
even though the S in the peso abbreviation and the S in the $ sign
both originally indicated the plural form.

After Mexican Independence the occasional use of the $ sign for
the Mexican peso began within Mexico as shown by a document
for "cinco mil pesos" dated October 1, 1822, with a clearly written conventional $ sign (fig. 7).

7

Differences in Value of Reals (Reales)

Some of the Fitzpatrick letters to merchants in Mobile and Pensacola in West Florida show that 10 reals were equal to one dollar in that region as well as in New Orleans instead of 8 reals to one dollar used by Fitzpatrick when he was in Manchac. This differential had arisen due to the minting in Iberian Spain, beginning in 1707, of a debased 2 real coinage and its fractions having about 20% less silver than prior coinage while generally retaining the same size by adulteration. The debased 2 real coin was called a "pistareen" but retained the 2 real denomination in its legend for many years thereafter. No such reduction in silver content took place in coinage in Spanish American mints. Much of the debased 2 real coinage naturally came to America replacing some of the full weight 2 real and other denominations in circulation. When this intrinsic value deficiency became a problem, American merchants had a choice of pricing less expensive items in reals at the rate of 8 to the dollar or adjusting prices to a 10 reals to the dollar basis. It depended upon whether pistareens were being accepted at their face value of 2 reals in small transactions or at a 20% discounted value. Some regions used one practice and some the other. This had the effect of complicating addition and multiplication for merchants doing business in regions using different money of account valuations. Once the dollar or peso total had been arrived at on either basis any payment in coin required discounting of only pistareens from their full value. The Fitzpatrick letterbooks elucidate the real to the dollar practice. For example "$881.8½ r" is written in a June 30, 1768 letter from New Orleans; "$187.9¼" is written in an April 13, 1769 letter from New Orleans; and "$260.8¼ rs" in a June 4, 1770 letter from Mobile. No letters have portions of a dollar written as 10 or more.

Totals with portions of a dollar exceeding 8 reals indicate the use of a 10 real ratio to the dollar. In letters sent from Manchac to Peter Swanson in Mobile dated May 31, 1770, and to Thomas Walters in Pensacola dated October 4, 1777, Fitzpatrick uses the expression "your money" to refer to a 10 reals to the dollar basis.

In a letter to John Ritson in Pensacola dated May 11, 1770, a calculation on the basis of 10 reals to the dollar is as follows with an unusual spelling of doubloons:

His honor. Elias Dunfords note for	$ 118.7 r	
Leut. Wm. Featherstons note	158.	
		$ 276.7 r

	11 Doubble Louns at $16	176.
in Gold	5 half Joes at 8½	42.5 r
	a light pistole	3.6 1/4
	In Silver	1.1 3/4
		223.3
		$ 500.

In a letter from Manchac to Mobile dated August 30, 1770, Fitzpatrick, using the word bit meaning real, stated as to shelled corn per barrel "I can have delivered me here at 10 bits this currency say 12½ bits your money ..." showing the differential in value of reals in the two regions. If a cash payment was made in a 10 real to the dollar region, full weight Spanish American 2 real coins should have been received at 4 to the dollar, but may sometimes have been improperly credited to a customer only at the rate of 5 pistareens to the dollar.

Oliver Pollock's Participation

In a five page invoice concerning many types of merchandise shipped from New Orleans on April 1, 1778, on board *Bateau La Providence*, by Oliver Pollock and consigned to Robert Morris, William Smith and Henry Laurens (the United States Secret Committee to Charter Vessels and Transport) "on Account & Risque of the United Independent States of America" in Philadelphia, there are two distinct positions in which the $ sign is placed.[10] The invoice is in English in the handwriting of a clerk and signed by Oliver Pollock personally. Data for each type of item included in each container is listed in a separate horizontal line as was customary. The number of pieces was entered first, then a description of the item, next the unit price of the item, followed by the aggregate charge for all of the same items. To the left of each unit price is the symbol a or @ for at. The unit price is in dollars except that if the unit price is less than a full dollar the price is listed in reals. The reals are abbreviated with r or R to the right of the numerals constituting the price in reals and the dollars are symbolized by a $ sign to the right of the numerals for the price in dollars. The subtotal of aggregate charges for the content of each container is set out in a line further to the right and a page total is at the bottom of those subtotals. The page total is carried forward to the top of the following page. Each page total and each carry forward total has a $ sign to the left of the numerals and punctuation at the end of the full amount of dollars. If a portion of a dollar results, that portion is entered in reals without further designation. The invoice contains 73 of the conventional $ signs.

The placement of the $ sign on the right side of numerals used for pricing and on the left side of numerals used for totals shows practicality as the motivation for so doing. The customary use of r or R for reals on the right side of a unit price when reals were the basis for that price avoided interference or confusion with the a or @. The $ was similarly placed on the right side of a price when price was equal to or exceeded one dollar. When totals were calculated the result was always in dollars and the $ sign was placed on the left side of the numerals to avoid confusion with a dollar amount which in many instances included a fractional part of a dollar expressed in reals. Since Spanish American silver coins in circulation had denominations only in reals (1/8th dollar per real for full weight pieces), punctuation was used to separate the whole dollar amounts from the reals in a total. Maravedis as a subdivision of reals were too insignificant to include but the occasional use of additional punctuation shows that the clerk had been accustomed to using maravedis.

Typical selected entries from the invoice follow with our parenthetical explanatory additions:

Amount Brought over		$ 4506..6.. ..
A trunk containing Vizs	(unit prices)	(line aggregate)
49 pieces Brittania	a 18 Rs	110..2.. ..
4 doz & 4 check shirt	a 18 $	78.. .. ..
2 pieces Corde	a 16 $	32.. .. ..
1 piece diaper		30.. .. ..
1 doz pair mens thread hose		9.. .. ..
Hair trunk & corde		4.. .. ..
(Container subtotal)		263..2.. ..
(Typical page total)	Carried over	$5629.2½

On July 6, 1778, Pollock wrote a letter from New Orleans to the Committee of Congress in Philadelphia containing a problem in the settlement of a Revolutionary War claim due from the United States as prize money for the capture of the British ship *Rebecca*. Pollock had offered the crew "$4750" and the crew insisted upon "ps 5500" (fig. 8).

8

The use of different symbols for the same matter may seem unusual, but it is similar to a Fitzpatrick letter dated May 9, 1771. The original Pollock letter is lost but is known from a copy made by a Philadelphia scribe on October 11, 1782, when such papers were forwarded to Congress.

In another portion of the copy of that July 6, 1778 letter the $ sign follows the numerals (fig. 9). In the Philadelphia scribe's copy

9

of an August 11, 1778 letter from Pollock to the Committee the $ sign is used in front of the numerals on several occasions (fig. 10).

10

In a September 11, 1778 Pollock letter to George Rogers Clark the $ sign is used but the letter is written by a Virginia scribe (fig. 11).

11

During the American Revolution, Oliver Pollock was working in New Orleans (then Spanish Territory) as a secret United States commercial agent. His biographer, James Alton James, infers that Pollock was a developer of the $ sign.[11] Pollock had come to America from Coleraine, Ireland, in 1760, at age 23. Backed by Willing and Morris of Philadelphia, in 1763, he became a ship operating trader headquartered in Havana, Cuba, dealing extensively in rum, coffee, flour, lumber, spices, slaves, etc., with merchants at east coast American ports. He became fluent in Spanish. In 1768 he moved his headquarters to New Orleans and established trade with other Gulf ports and the Mississippi Valley. When Alejandro O'Reilly came to New Orleans on August 17, 1769, in a second Spanish attempt to administer the region, he needed a substantial amount of flour and

Pollock supplied it at normal prices instead of opportunistically increasing his profit by raising prices. This action put Pollock in a favored position for the future there. When the American Revolution began Pollock furnished the Americans with information and supplies and helped to keep Spain cooperating with the Americans.

James, who was familiar with the Fitzpatrick letterbooks, construes Fitzpatrick's $ signs as transitional rather than a true $ sign. However the letter dated January 20, 1780, from Pollock to Congress is definitely written by Pollock personally and shows that Pollock himself was using a transitional form (fig. 12).

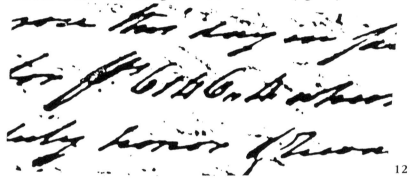

12

In a September 18, 1782 letter from Pollock to Congress handwritten by a scribe but signed by Pollock and obviously composed by Pollock, "Dollars" is used after numerals 14 times, "Drs" is used after a number once but nowhere is the $ sign used. Whether in one distinctive form or another, whether original or a copy, whether by the writer or by a scribe, the important point is that the receiver of any such communication at the time understood what the sender meant by using the $ sign. Fitzpatrick had already written to Pollock on December 1, 1775, using the $ sign once and on October 1, 1776, using the $ sign on 4 occasions. The previously described invoice of April 1, 1778, written by Pollock's clerk, shows fully developed uniform $ signs. Apparently in 1937, when James's book about Pollock was published, James was unaware of the use of the $ sign by Ezra L'Hommedieu of New York in 1776 (as disclosed in articles by Cajori in 1913 through 1929), and any claim on behalf of Pollock as the first user of the conventional $ sign lacks support. Since Fitzpatrick, Pollock and many others had been sending and receiving trade documents and correspondence in great quantity using the $ sign in recognizable form, they must all be given credit for developing its practicality and its eventual general acceptance.

The $ Sign Shifts Position

Among the incomplete records of William Constable & Co., a New York trading partnership organized May 10, 1784, there remain some letters written in 1786 addressed to merchants in Philadelphia, West Indies ports and elsewhere which use the $ sign following the numerals in amounts of money and in no instance in front of the numerals. In 1787 the $ sign sometimes appears in front of and sometimes following such numerals. By 1789 the $ sign is always used in front of the numerals. Whether written by scribes or by the principals or both this evolution of the positioning of the $ sign shows the timing of its change of position by commercial Americans just becoming accustomed to using it. They were going through the same thinking and practices which John Fitzpatrick and others had experienced elsewhere.

The Chalk as a Money of Account

Daniel McGillivray was an independent operator as well as an agent for other firms in trading with native Americans in the East Florida and West Florida areas during the last quarter of the eighteenth century. His wife was a native American of the Creek tribe, enabling him to furnish extensive information to the British, United States and Spanish authorities as to the thinking and practices of the Creeks and other tribes as well as to trade extensively with them in furs and other items. His surviving account book lists prices in "chalks" during the 1788-90 period and when he converts "chalk" totals into dollars and reals he uses the $ sign. Selected entries are as follows:

> 58 chalks in goods @ 3 rs ... 21..6
> 414 chalks reduced to dollars is $ 155..3
> 738 chalks reduced to dollars $ is 276..6

The chalk was equivalent for trading purposes to one pound weight of dressed deerskin which was valued in full weight coin at 3 reals (3/8ths dollar or 37.5 cents). Prices and accounts in trading with the Creek tribe were kept in chalks. This expression was obviously introduced to the Creek and other tribes in the area by English traders who were accustomed to making a tally by chalking one up on a slate or skin or by making tally marks with a stick on the ground. In two of the above entries the English word dollars was first written out and then followed with a $ sign, showing that the writer was calculating in dollars and reals. He was not using decimal calculations since his parts of a dollar were in reals. It can be noted that the $ sign is used in two different positions.

The First Printed Dollar Symbol

In the past there has been a broad difference of opinion on the source of the printed form of the true or conventional $ sign. This has occurred primarily because some printed items had not yet been located and certain historical data as to American type founders had been misapplied.

Lee's *The American Accomptant*, published in 1797, contained the earliest known illustration of a United States coin in its frontispiece.[12] The book proposed five different symbols for monetary amounts to be used for commercial instruction in reckoning in Federal money. These symbols were referred to by the author as "characteristics." The mill was represented by a straight line running on a diagonal from upper right to lower left, being virtually identical with the then existing English symbol for shilling. The symbol for the cent was created by adding another straight line of equal length running on a diagonal parallel with and close to the line representing the mill. For the dime symbol a thick undulating stroke from upper left to lower right was added diagonally across the center of the two parallel lines used as the symbol for the cent, the top end of the undulating stroke pointing vertically upward and the bottom end of the stroke pointing vertically downward.

For the dollar symbol the two parallel lines used for the cent symbol were retained as a base but a complex element from the upper left to the lower right was superimposed across the center of the cent lines in similar placement to the undulating stroke used on the dime symbol. That complex element in the dollar symbol resembles the outline of a short earthworm with its top end pointing vertically upward and its bottom end pointing vertically downward. The designation for Ten Dollars (officially known as an Eagle) was merely the abbreviation E (figs. 13-15).

All of these symbols were used in the calculating exercises in Lee's book after an explanation of them on page 56, but in later pages the dollar symbol is retained and the others are sparsely used. There are altogether 232 uses of the dollar symbol, as many as 8 being found on one page. There is no evidence that any of Lee's symbol system was ever used before or after the publication of his book. Lee's use of multiple symbols seems to have been substantially influenced by the £, s, d, and f, representing the pound, shilling, pence and farthing in the British-style money of account systems used in the American colonies and in Lee's time still used to a great extent in the American states. Although Lee was very enthusiastic about the decimal system he did not take into consideration the fact that

Of Federal Money.

Characteristics.

10 Mills (/) make	1 Cent.		//
10 Cents - - -	1 Dime.		X
10 Dimes - -	1 Dollar.		X
10 Dollars - -	1 Eagle.*		E.

13

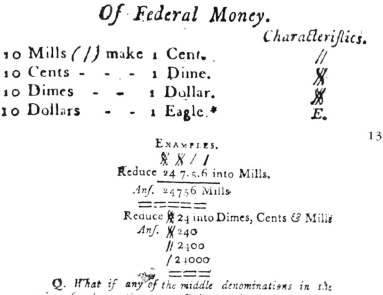

EXAMPLES.

X X / /

Reduce 24 7.5.6 into Mills.

Anf. 24756 Mills.

Reduce X 24 into Dimes, Cents & Mills

Anf. X 240

// 2400

/ 24000

Q. *What if any of the middle denominations in the given fum be wanting, as 5 Dollars and 5 Mills?*

A. Fill each and all of the vacant denominations with Cyphers; thus X 5.00.5 and then reduce as before.

14

Q **H**OW *do you fubtract Federal Money?*

A. The rule of operation and of proof, in this and all the other Federal Tables following, is precifely the fame as that of whole numbers, obferving only to keep the denominationns diftinct by the feperating Points.

	1	2	3
	X / /	X // /	X // /
From	17.35 5	175.75 0	571.57 4
Take	15.31 3	142.95 5	523.65 9
Rem.	2.14 2		

	4	5	6
	X // /	X //	X // /
Borr.	43.6 4 3	59.7 4	48.3 3 3
Paid	37.9 3 7	43.8 3	22.6 6 6
Due			

15

under decimalization the official U.S. monetary units and the coins minted accordingly would eliminate the need for more than one fundamental monetary symbol accompanying the numerals. Lee's system was thus conceptually obsolete, impractical and very difficult to transcribe.

It is obvious that Lee's monetary symbols were conceived by adding one line or stroke for each larger decimal unit so that the dollar symbol was composed of four separate lines or strokes. His dollar symbol seems to have had no relationship to the handwritten conventional $ sign which had already been in use by some merchants, bookkeepers and others for as long as 30 years in scattered parts of colonial America and subsequently the United States.

Lee's symbol for the dollar was called to the attention of the numismatic public in *The Numismatist* for September 1899[13] and generally accepted as the first printed use of the conventional dollar sign until 1925 when Professor Florian Cajori challenged it.

An examination of Lee's symbols, particularly his dollar symbol, shows that they were original with him and that he was not familiar with the existing conventional $ sign. Such a conclusion is reached by noting that the curving portions of his dollar symbol do not conform to the Roman S in the conventional $ sign or to the old English long s. The upper end of a Roman S always points either horizontally or downward and not vertically upward as Lee's strokes do. The lower end of a Roman S always points either horizontally or upward and not vertically downward as Lee's strokes do. A Roman S is made with one stroke and not with two separate strokes joining at each end and leaving a long enclosed area between them. The old English long s slopes from upper right to lower left, greatly differing from Lee's two curving strokes sloping in an opposite direction. It seems proper to conclude that Lee would have been pleased to include the conventional $ sign as his dollar symbol if he had been aware of it. He would have been intellectually dishonest as an instructor and writer if he had known about the conventional $ sign and had concealed that fact from those he wished to teach. His dollar symbol could not have been a partial modification of the conventional $ sign because his symbol for the dime resembled the conventional $ sign more closely than his dollar symbol as Cajori stated. The worm-like element in Lee's dollar symbol cannot be easily handwritten but must be tediously and carefully drawn and spaced to be read and to be distinguishable from his symbol for the dime.

Thus it seems proper to exclude Lee's dollar symbol from being designated as the first printed use of the conventional $ sign because there is no evidence that either was derived from or influenced by the other. Granted he was the first to develop a symbol for the dollar in type form rather than spelling out "dollar" or employing an abbreviation, but it appears to be an isolated concept, unrelated to the prior handwritten $ sign.

The maker of the type for Lee's symbols remains unknown. Christopher Sauer (Sower) began his print shop in 1772 in Germantown, Pennsylvania which was sold to his assistant, Justus Fox in 1784. Fox cast limited styles of type as did Jacob Bey, another assistant who later operated independently. Neither was engaged in that operation by 1797. John Baine from Scotland attempted some typefounding in Philadelphia beginning in 1787 and by 1797 had gone out of business as had Adam Gerard Mappa from Holland who similarly operated in New York beginning in 1790. Henry Lewis Bullen in 1919 had speculated that:

> In 1797 Archibald Binny was the only punch cutter in the U.S. and doubtless cut the punches for Dr. Lee's monetary sign. B & R (Binny & Ronaldson) was not satisfied with the sign made for Lee's book. Binny redesigned the character.[14]

This statement had no factual support. Binny had come to America from Scotland in 1793 skilled in punch cutting and matrix making for typecasting and set up in Philadelphia in 1796 for the purpose of casting type. His products were uniform and far superior to the symbols used in Lee's book.

Updike's *Printing Types* (1922) repeated Bullen's 1919 thoughts and stated:

> Many of these small equipments finally fell into the hands of two Scotchmen, Archibald Binny and James Ronaldson, whose Philadelphia foundry was begun in 1796. In 1797, they offered for sale the first dollar - marks ever made in type.[15]

P.J. Conkwright pointed out in 1955 that this Updike comment was inaccurate and was apparently copied from *1796-1896 One Hundred Years, MacKellar, Smiths and Jordan Foundry*, a centennial celebration publication in 1896 of American typefounding by Thomas MacKellar, which stated:

> Binny & Ronaldson first began to manufacture the dollar mark in 1797 and under date of November 13, of the same year, it appears on Page 2 of Ledger A for the first time.[16]

An examination of that Binny & Ronaldson ledger by Conkwright showed that the dollar mark referred to was handwritten as a ledger entry and there was no evidence whatever that it was available in type. Certainly the remarks by MacKellar were restated by Bullen and Updike based upon the existence of the dollar symbol in Lee's book. No other use of type for any symbol for the dollar during or prior to 1797 was then or is now known.

The earliest printing which Conkwright had located by 1955 for the use of the conventional $ sign in type was on January 2, 1802, in the *Aurora*, a Philadelphia newspaper printed by William Duane. This is over four years after Lee's publication. Unfortunately there are no known type foundry specimen sheets containing any $ sign until E. White & Co. (Elihu White) of New York in 1812 showed a conventional $ sign for sale on his sheet. Binny & Ronaldson did not list the $ sign in *A Specimen of Metal Ornaments* (Philadelphia 1809) where the prices were even spelled out as "dollars" nor did they include it in their specimen book of 1812. D. & G. Bruce of New York City offered type for the conventional $ sign in 1815. Finally James Ronaldson of Philadelphia who had bought out Binny offered 10 different sizes of the conventional $ sign for sale in 1816 in his specimen sheets. The omission of the conventional $ sign in a specimen sheet does not indicate that it was not available. Conkwright pointed out that in the foundry equipment of Binny & Ronaldson there actually was a matrix to cast type for the identical $ sign used beginning in 1802 to print the Philadelphia newspaper *Aurora*. This original copper matrix was retained by American Type Founders' Company and is presently at the National Museum of American History. The recent discovery of the use in 1799 of type from this identical matrix is explained subsequently.

It was also asserted by Conkwright in 1955 that each of Lee's printed dollar symbols differs from the others in size and shape. He also claimed that each piece of type used to print them was separately engraved. It is obvious that they were not cast in type metal from a matrix or they would all be virtually identical. They are crudely done. If each piece of type for the dollar symbol had been separately engraved it would have been a most laborious task and most impractical. The same would have been true for the dime symbol.

An examination of the several type fonts used in setting the general text of Lee's book indicates that the type he used was purchased from London, England, as proven by an examination of the 1788 *Specimen of Printing Types* by Edmund Fry and Co. Fry also had many ornaments and insignia for sale but not any of Lee's money symbols. Wands, as printer of Lee's book, had been in the printing business in Lansingburgh since at least 1792 (Tiffany & Wands was the printer of circulating scrip in 1792 issued by the Lansingburgh

Museum) and it was then customary for American printers to buy their type from European sources. If Wands had obtained the unusual symbols for Lee from a European type founder they would have been uniform but the expense and delay of such a special order would have made it impractical. Thus he seems to have found another way to create them.

The handwritten entries in the 1797-1801 ledgers of Binny & Ronaldson list 144 different customers for type throughout the United States and William W. Wands is not among them.

There are 232 dollar insignia in the Wands printing of Lee's 312 page book. The size is duodecimo (about 7″ × 4″). It would have been customary for some of the type for the dollar insignia and other unique insignia to be reused just as other type would have been reused in setting a book printed in parts. The printed collation or signature marks used on the pages to guide the binder in the signature assembly of Lee's book are alternatively every 4 and 8 pages (A followed by A1; B followed by B1; etc.), making it clear that 12 pages were first printed in one impression on a single sheet. When that sheet was rotated 180 degrees on its central axis, another impression would be made on the other side so that there would be two identical sets of 12 pages on the sheet. This sheet was cut in half and each half cut into unequal parts for customary folding into 4 and 8 page alternating sections. Thus when the scheduled number of a sheet impression was printed, the type could be released and reused in setting further text. The maximum number of dollar insignia in any 12 page impression was 20 (pages 228 through 240) and if reused no more were required. If type for another 12 page impression was being set while the prior 12 page make-up was in press, then more type would have had to be on hand. The question left unanswered is how 20 or more different pieces of type for the dollar insignia and a lesser number of different pieces for the dime insignia were prepared in a way which resulted in all of them being somewhat different. The special insignia could have been cast in molds which often broke after each lead pouring. This might be true of clay or plaster molds which still retained some moisture after drying and usually cracked from the heat of the hot type metal. This was the problem Benjamin Franklin had encountered in inventing nature printing in 1737 and by William Ged of Edinburgh, Scotland, in trying to perfect stereotyping in 1739.

If each soft mold had been formed with one punch carved out of wood or lead the resulting cast insignia would be generally uniform. If each soft mold would have been formed with the use of more than one punch, variances would occur. Pieces of cast type on hand could have been modified to make two or more punches for the different parts of Lee's dollar insignia. The use of available cast type would also give a standard depth to any such impression in clay or plaster.

A possibility for such punches is the modification of the section mark (§) which has a worm-like central portion with pointed or rounded ends and curled tails at the top and bottom. It was routinely sold by English typecasters to American printers during the eighteenth century. In addition to its normal use it was also used for borders and decorations. Paper money printed on behalf of American colonies and independent states such as Virginia, North Carolina and Maryland has many such marks, the 15 shilling and £3 denominations of the North Carolina issue of April 23, 1761, each having a total of 83 of such § marks divided into two sizes. The tails and other portions of the section marks could easily have been cut off or filed off such cast type to form one or more punches to be used to form the worm-like portion of Lee's dollar insignia. Then an additional piece of cast type containing a line or parallel lines could be used diagonally so as to form the balance of Lee's dollar insignia in the soft mold. A number of such molds could be made at one time prior to drying and pouring or could have been made as needed depending upon mold fracturing. Wands as printer could have undertaken a project of this nature in his shop.

While it may be unscientific to speculate on what caused the individual differences in the dollar and other monetary insignia used in Lee's book, the omission of such suggested possibilities might be neglectful. Further findings in this regard can hopefully be anticipated.

The First Printed Conventional $ Sign

In a pamphlet entitled *Facts Respecting the Bank of North America*,[17] there are 14 printed conventional $ signs in identical form and followed by numerals. This eight-page pamphlet is undated and without an indicated author. The $ sign has two very close diagonal parallel strokes tilting from upper right to lower left across a well-formed S (fig. 16). The date of the printing of the pamphlet must be determined from its content.

The Pennsylvania charter of the reincorporated Bank of North America was to expire on March 17, 1801, unless further extended by a Pennsylvania enactment. The text of the pamphlet covers the history of the Bank of North America, describing its patriotic assistance to the Federal government and its loans to the State of necessary sum was not subscribed until December, 1781 ; and, even at that late period, the actual amount of monies paid in by individual Subscribers did not exceed $ 85,000. In order to encourage the Bank, the Superintendant of Finance subscribed, on account of the United States, for Stock to the amount of $ 250,000 ; but the Finances were so much exhausted, that, in the December following, the Bank was obliged to release the United States from their subscription, to the amount of $ 200,000 ; the remaining $ 50,000 having been sold, by the Superintendant, to some persons in Holland.

16

Pennsylvania in 1782, 1791 and 1792. The pamphlet states that there is no reason for the dissolution of the Bank and that "it may not be improper to make some observations on the application for a renewal of the charter" and "when the Legislature is informed of these services and of the great number of citizens interested in the institution, it is hoped they will grant a renewal of the charter ...."

The records show that the initial motion to extend the Bank's charter was submitted to the Pennsylvania House of Representatives in Philadelphia on February 5, 1799. Legislation to extend the charter for 14 additional years was fully enacted and approved by March 20, 1799. The pamphlet would only have been useful if printed between those dates. It would not have been printed earlier because it refers to the "application" for renewal of the charter.

The pamphlet was separately printed in Harrisburg, Pennsylvania by John Wyeth, and in Lancaster, Pennsylvania by William Dickson (Dixon). The text is exactly the same in each. The type used in each pamphlet was set independently from completely different type fonts except for the $ signs which were type cast from a single or identical brass matrix. Wyeth capitalizes the first "A" of America in "Bank of North America", while Dickson uses a hyphen after "North" and a lower case "a" in "america." The pamphlets show some variances in line breaks. No other printings of this pamphlet are known, particularly none were from Philadelphia.

There must have been a good reason for these two virtually identical printings. The Philadelphia business interests were naturally in favor of the Bank continuing. The affirmative vote of the rural legislators was needed for passage. John Wyeth published a newspaper (*The Oracle of Dauphin*) in Harrisburg and had distribution capabilities in that part of the state. William Dickson, a politically active printer in Lancaster (which was about to become the new capital of Pennsylvania), had a different range of contacts. Each printer would therefore be able to reach different groups. It would not be politically tactful to ask either printer to distribute something printed by another printer. The removal of the capital of the State of Pennsylvania from Philadelphia to Lancaster was then under consideration and was approved in Philadelphia on April 4, 1799. The first legislative session in Lancaster took place on November 5, 1799. This indicated the political importance of Dickson's selection for printing the pamphlets he distributed.

The fact that identical well formed $ signs are found in each printing points to the nearby type founders, Binny & Ronaldson, of Philadelphia, whose steel punched brass matrix of that identical $ sign still exists. This is further confirmed by handwritten Binny & Ronaldson ledger entries of the 1796-1801 period where both Wyeth and Dixon are separately listed as customers. No Philadelphia newspaper or other American publication appears to have used any $ sign in print prior to the 1799 pamphlets, so that date of February 1799 may be accepted as the first printed use of a conventional $ sign until new facts may show otherwise.

The earliest use of the Binny & Ronaldson $ sign heretofore pointed out by others has been in the Philadelphia newspaper *Aurora*, for January 2, 1802, on page 2, column 5. In a further perusal of that newspaper, it is found that the $ sign was first used in the issue of December 18, 1801, in three instances (fig. 17). In

NEW ORLEANS.
Cotton per cwt. 28 dollars ; tobacco, per do. 4 dollars ; bar iron per do. 35 dollars ; bacon per do. 12 dollars 50 cents ; salted pork per barrel 14 dollars ; flour per do. 10 dollars ; whiskey per gallon, 75 cents ; peach brandy per do. 1 dollar 50 cents ; corn unshell'd per bushel 1 dollar.

———

Prices at Havanna, 32 days since.
Lumber, $34 ; pork $ 30 ; beef 20 a 29 ; other provisions plenty—flour $ 9 ; molasses and sugar scarce.

17

the *Aurora* for January 2, 1802, there was a U.S. Treasury report containing "dollars" spelled out 38 times and the $ sign was used only 2 times. There was no shortage of $ sign type because 22 such

2,982 perch. Lock chamber in common stone *a* 3 $\frac{10}{100}$ $ 10,262
1,579 do. Above in ashler *a* 5 $ 7,895
2,240 do. Gate and sluice walls to
upper locks, *a* 4 $ 8,960
1,579 do. Lock chamber below
high water, *a* 3 $\frac{50}{100}$ $ 5,226 18

insignia were used in the January 7, 1802 *Aurora* issue (fig. 18). All of these $ signs are identical to the $ sign used in *Facts Respecting the Bank of North America*. William Duane, printer of the *Aurora*, is also on the customer list of Binny & Ronaldson. On November 13, 1802, the same $ sign was used in *The Gazette of the United States* (Philadelphia) and in the *New York Herald* of June 1802, for lottery prizes. All of these are type from the Binny & Ronaldson matrix.

It seems very curious that the casting of type for printing the $ sign in 1799 took place before any special type for printing the English £ sign had been cast anywhere, even though the £ sign had been used in printing in Great Britain and elsewhere long beforehand. The printing of the £ sign had been accomplished by inverting a Janson style J as shown in fig. 19. This inversion can be observed on the 1757 paper money printed in and issued by the colonies of North Carolina and Virginia from Janson type imported from Britain.

This is an example of a type called *Janson* and this is how the *J* can be turned upside down to make a pound sign: £25 15*s* 6*d*   19

Governmental Use of the $ Sign on Money and Loans

When the Spanish dollar was adopted as a monetary unit for paper money issues of the Colony of Maryland in 1767, by the Continental Congress in 1775, and by most of the individual States during the Revolutionary War and Confederation period, there were no $ signs used on the currency. The dollar monetary unit was always expressed in lettering reading DOLLAR(S) or an abbreviation of it, whether type set, engraved into a printing plate or in a cut or block inserted into a printing form. No dollar coinage was issued by any of those governments prior to the adoption of the U.S. Constitution in 1789 except the pattern or trial strikings of 1776 Continen-

tal Currency Coinage of one dollar which did not have any
denomination or monetary unit in its legends and the 1783 Nova
Constellatio silver pattern of Robert Morris which had 1000 mills
or units as its denomination. Massachusetts in 1787 and 1788 struck
copper cents and half cents, but these denominations used the word
CENT and had no reason to refer to the dollar.

The official loan documents of the Continental Congress and the
individual states for the period of the American Revolution and until the adoption of the U.S. Constitution were sometimes in dollars
or Spanish dollars and whether handwritten, typeset, or engraved
none have been located which contain a printed or handwritten $
sign. In such obligations and documents the amount was customarily
in handwritten form in the text and was often duplicated elsewhere
on the document in numerical form for convenience.

In a January 20, 1791 typeset printed receipt form of the U.S.
Commissioner of Loans in Boston, the amount of the obligation in
the primary text is filled in with handwritten numerals without any
designation of dollars or cents other than a handwritten dash between them. There is a typeset combining symbol printed as an alteration protector to the left of the space for the handwritten numbers.
When the numbers are totalled below in handwritten numerals
within printed horizontal lines the word "Dollars" is printed well
to the left of the handwritten numerals and no alteration protection symbol is used (fig. 20).

20

The earliest use located for the $ sign on an American govern-
mental obligation is found on a partially engraved, partially typeset
and partially handwritten United States Loan Office certificate issued
January 17, 1792 to "George Washington of Fairfax County,

Virginia'' in the amount of ''One Hundred & Eighty five dollars &
Ninety eight cents Assumed Debt.'' The quoted portions are handwritten. In the lower left corner the amount is repeated in hand-
writing as ''$ 185'' followed first by ''Dollars'' printed from an
engraved block and then by a handwritten '' & 98 Cts.'' The $ sign
is written with a single upright (fig. 21).

21

Most subsequent United States Loan Office certificates, where the
amount is required to be written in, also have a repetition of the
amount in written numerical form in the lower left corner with the
word DOLLARS printed in an engraved ornamental frame. When
the amount is handwritten to the left of the ornamental frame, an
alteration protector is often used—one to the left of the numerals
to protect that side and sometimes one to the right of the word
DOLLARS so an amount in cents cannot be added. These alteration
protector marks are usually a handwritten '' # '' (the symbol for
number or pound weight) or a dash or one or more crosses or curves.
The $ sign usage in this context was minimal because DOLLARS was
already printed on the form (figs. 22-24).

22

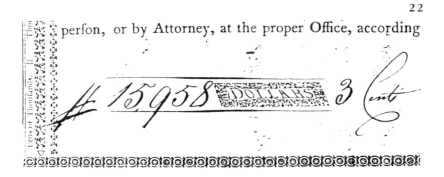

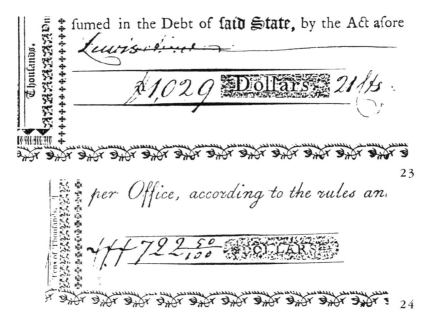

Continuing into the first decade of the nineteenth century, the United States obligations authorized by the various Acts of Congress were in similar form but for convenience, pursuant to certain authorizations, specific denominations were printed on the obligation document and not filled in by hand. In such case the amount and the word DOLLARS were printed in typeset letters, but in the lower left corner area, typeset numerals were used, DOLLARS spelled out in typeset letters, and a typeset alteration protector printed in front of the numerals.

In an August 27, 1800 obligation for "1000 Dollars," the alteration protector in the lower left corner is a typeset "§" or section sign (fig. 25).

In a January 11, 1805 obligation for "400 Dollars," the protector consists of two identical typeset ornaments, each with a worm-like form slanting down to the left and an interrupted diagonal line slanting down to the right (fig. 26; this ornament somewhat resembles in mirror image an element in the Chauncey Lee dollar symbol of 1797).

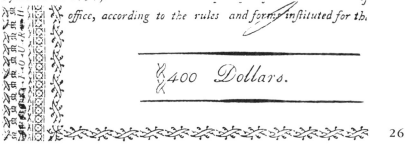

26

In a May 13, 1806 obligation for "400 Dollars," the alteration protector consists of three typeset 8 pointed star-like ornaments as points of a triangle known in printing as an asterism (fig. 27).

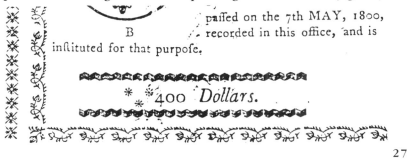

27

For the 1813 U.S. Loan, the lower left corner of the obligation has the word DOLLARS in typeset letters moved to the left of the space to be filled in by handwritten numerals. By this action the right end of the numerals required alteration protection by writing in some mark by hand (fig. 28).

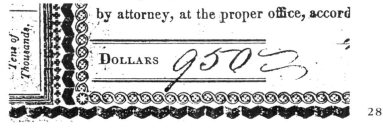

28

This practice continued for more than another decade even though check writing, invoicing, accounting records and private obligations had solved this alteration problem with a $ sign to the left and a fraction line or punctuation to the right of the written dollar numerals.

The various typeset styles and ornament placements on U.S. fiscal obligations, at a time when type for the $ sign was readily available beginning in 1799, indicates that there was a reluctance to accept the $ sign on formal or official documents. It was not until U.S. obligations were privately designed and printed by Rawdon, Wright & Hatch from fully engraved plates under the Act of October 12, 1837, that the use of the printed $ sign on some of the formal U. S. obligations was commenced and continued at convenience.

At the commencement of the Civil War, in addition to issuing bonds, the Union authorized and issued interest bearing, circulating notes of appropriate size and denomination. A design submitted for the back of an 1861 Interest Bearing Note of 500 dollars contained a warning that the fine for counterfeiting was "$1000" in addition to confinement. In due course the Union issued various types of non-interest bearing paper money for circulation and when a counterfeit warning was placed on some National Bank Notes in 1863, the $ sign was similarly applied. Beginning in 1869, many Legal Tender or United States Notes had a $ sign in the counterfeit warning.

The use of the $ sign on the back of the Compound Interest Notes of 1863, etc., was used as part of the total amount of interest payable. The $ sign then spread to coupons as a space saver. The first instance of a $ sign as a major element in the design of circulating Federal currency is on some of the Coin Notes of the Series of 1890 and 1891.

However a decorative emblem of a capital S superimposed on the right upright of a capital U was extensively used on federally authorized paper money beginning in the Civil War period and continuing into the twentieth century. That emblem does not resemble a $ sign but if its S portion had been centered over both uprights of the U it would have appeared similar. The emblem is merely an artistic "U S" insignia. It is found 15 times on the 1875 series $20 U.S. Note and a lesser number of times on other denominations. It is used either on the face or back or both. It is found on various issues and denominations of Interest Bearing Treasury Notes, Compound Interest Notes, Legal Tender or U.S. Notes, Coin Notes, Silver Certificates, Gold Certificates, and National Bank Notes. It seems to have developed independently as a design element without any influence from the prior existence of the conventional $ sign.

Other Early Printed $ Sign Uses

W. Stillman engraved a promissory note form for the Washington Bank in Westerly, Rhode Island. It is hand dated July 14, 1803. Apparently through inexperience, the engraver created a mirror image $ sign but each S is properly cut into the engraved plate. Nevertheless that $ sign is the earliest engraved $ sign which has been located (fig. 29).

29

The mirror image of a large $ sign again evidenced itself during the Civil War when M. Mayers & Bro., druggists at Fort Smith, Arkansas, put into circulation $1 scrip notes dated December 18, 1861, printed in part from wooden type (fig. 30).

30

In the Harrisburg, Pennsylvania newspaper *Oracle of Dauphin*, for January 17, 1807, there are four methods of presenting monetary units for prices, (1) only an indicator for cents, (2) a $ sign, (3) the abbreviations of dls and dl, and (4) no monetary indicator at all, each method being aided by appropriate spacing between the numerals for dollars and the numerals for cents (fig. 31).

| Belmour, a novel, 2 vols. 2 25cts.
| Betham's Biographical Dictionary
| of celebrated women of every
| age and country, . 8 2 50
| Life of Erasmus. 6 dls.
| Goldsmith's Essays, 2 vols. 1 dl.
| 50 cents.
| Scott's Dissertations, essays and
| parellels, 2 33

31

There was a slow introduction of the conventional $ sign in books, possibly fearing a hesitant public acceptance. The first edition (1801) of *The Scholar's Arithmetic or Federal Accountant*, devoted pages 87 through 97 to explanations and calculations involving Federal money.[18] When the text mentioned U.S. dollars they were referred to either as "Dollars" or "Dolls," capitalized or uncapitalized. This was also true in 1802 for the second edition. However in the third edition of that book published in 1805 in Leominister, Massachusetts, and thereafter until the final edition in 1833, the conventional $ sign was used extensively, particularly when amounts were tabulated or totalled. In 1808, other American reckoners, almanacs, instructional books and manuals on arithmetic, accounting and business calculations also began to use the $ sign, always trailing by several years the use of the printed $ sign in newspapers and other more informal documents.[19]

Elements of Arithmetic, published in 1823, seems to be the earliest book in the Louisiana Purchase portion of the United States using the printed $ sign routinely in applicable calculations.[20]

The use of the $ sign on printed checks slowly developed as people recognized the advantage of using the $ sign as an alteration pro-

CASHIER of the BANK.

Pay to

Dollars

Doll.

32

tector on the left side of a number. In the late eighteenth century, there was no such protection and either Doll, Dolls or Dollars were customarily printed on checks in a position so that numerals could be written in on the left and a fraction bar printed on the right (fig. 32)

On the early nineteenth century checks, the word "Dollars" was often printed at the left end so that the written numerals could be written in to the right of "Dollars" (fig. 33).

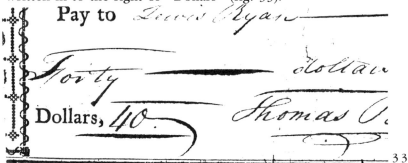

This was then changed by printing "Dollars" on the left, leaving a modest space to the right for written numerals and printing "cents" to the right of that space (fig. 34).

In an alternate form, "Dollars" was printed so that numerals could be written in to its left and a space followed by the printed word "cents" on the right of "Dollars" (fig. 35).

Sometimes a fraction bar with "100" underneath it was printed followed by "Dollars" in print so that the numerals for dollars could be written to the left and the numerals for cents written over the bar of the printed items. Fig. 36 ilustrates a check where a written $ sign is added as an alteration protector. In similar fashion a printed

36

37

$ sign was added to the left of the space for the numerals (fig. 37).

These were the early forms of checks which gave rise to the need to use the $ sign in expressing a monetary amount in a concise and protective manner.

The Portuguese $

When Portuguese inflation resulted in the circulation of high denomination bank notes beginning in 1797, that issue of paper money contained a $ as a symbol. In order to make the denominations of the engraved currency easier for the public to read, the $ was placed between the numerals constituting thousands and the numerals less than one thousand. For example 10,000 reis was printed as 10$000 rs and 2,400 reis was printed as 2$400 reis (figs. 38-39). This practice was continued on some Portuguese and Brazilian paper money during the nineteenth century when denominations were in multiples of milreis (1000 reis).

38

39

When in the eighth century Arabs moved westward across North Africa into the Iberian peninsula, they introduced their use of a zero in numbering. This was a symbol which Roman numerals did not include. This zero was called sifir in Arabic and cifra in Spanish and Portuguese. It was a representation of a mathematical concept or a code just as were other Arabic and Roman symbols for numbers and gave rise to the English word "cipher" which is understood as meaning number as well as code.

When Roman numerals were used to write a large number there often was a signal to represent thousand and this was a very wide M (the Roman letter representing 1000) or a convex arc which was written over the top of the Roman letter symbols which denoted the number of thousands (fig. 40). The Arabs simplified this indicator

40. Portugal, 16,252 (1497)

for writing both Roman and Arabic numbers by placing a long armed U between the symbols or numerals for one or more thousands
and those for less than one thousand (figs. 41-42). This long armed
U was stylistically written with flourishes so that by the beginning
of the eighteenth century in Portugal, it appeared as a U with arms
curving inward, over which a crossbar was sometimes added to
distinguish it as a symbol (fig. 43).

41. Castile, Spain
64,454 (1493)

42. Lisbon (1554)

43. Lisbon (1709)

44. Portugal (1711)

Lisbon (1761)

As its convenience further developed, the rounded U was improv-
ed by being divided into three parts by inscribing two close parallel
lines across it running from upper right to lower left. Thus the
rounded U was divided into three sections, one representing each
of the three numerals which were necessary to reach the thousand
plateau (fig. 44).

This aggrandizement or enlargement of the cifra or symbol for
thousand was then referred to in Portuguese as cifrão (phonetically
cifron) in accordance with the common Portuguese practice to add
a suffix in this manner to aggrandize the expression. After the middle of the eighteenth century, some stylistic modifications to the
rounded portion of the cifrão took place so that it appeared more
like an S than a modified U. The two parallel lines in the cifrão were
changed to a more nearly upright position. No items printed in Portuguese have been located which bear the cifrão $ symbol prior to
the year 1797 when the $ symbol was engraved into the plates for
printing Portuguese bank notes previously described.

The Portuguese kept the cifrão in common usage as a symbol for
thousand throughout the nineteenth century in both Portugal and
Brazil, but occasionally the style changed when the S portion
sometimes became topless, being a throw back to its origin as a
rounded U (figs. 45-47).

45. Vertical lines project (1888)

46. Vertical lines confined (1887)

47. Topless (1867-69)

An abrupt change in the meaning of the Portuguese $ symbol or cifrão occurred when a Portuguese decree of May 22, 1911, and the law of June 21, 1913, provided that the $ or cifrão no longer represented 1000 in monetary matters but thereafter was to represent a newly revived monetary unit, the Escudo. The Escudo was divided into 100 centavos. The newly defined $ symbol was placed between the number of Escudos and the number of centavos for monetary convenience, with the numerals to the left of the symbol representing Escudos and two numerals to the right representing the number of centavos. The new $ was also usable on the left end of the numbers and a punctuation mark or space used as a separator from centavos. These uses are evident on some twentieth century issues of Portuguese paper money (figs. 48-49).

48. (1920)

49. (1922)

Thus the Portuguese cifrão or $ symbol seems to have developed quite independently and for its entire lifetime has had an entirely separate meaning and interpretation from that of the conventional $ sign for dollar. No evidence has as yet come to our attention by which the Portuguese cifrão $ symbol influenced the conventional $ sign for dollar or vice versa.

The World Adopts the $ Sign

Those in the English speaking areas of Spanish regions in America would have little reason to believe that their form of $ sign would spread throughout the world (fig. 50). Their $ sign evolved to represent the United States dollar. Their $ sign was adopted by many nations which used the peso. Their $ sign was chosen to represent the dollar or other monetary unit of nations throughout the world including Australia, Bahamas, Barbados, Belize, Brazil, Canada, Cayman Islands, Chile, China, Columbia, Cuba, Dominica, Ethiopia, Guiana, Honduras, Hong Kong, Jamaica, Liberia, Malaysia, Mexico, New Zealand, Nicaragua, Peru, Philippines, Singapore, Taiwan, Trinidad, Uruguay and Vietnam.[21]

50

[1]   The amount of enthusiastic and excellent cooperation I have received from others
for this study is far in excess of assistance I have received in prior research. I needed
it. My utmost thanks go to Elizabeth M. Nuxoll as Project Editor of *The Papers of
Robert Morris*, Phil Lapsansky of the Library Company of Philadelphia, and Margaret
Fisher Dalrymple as author of *The Letterbooks of John Fitzpatrick 1768-1790*. To
Leslie Elam as Director of the American Numismatic Society for his constant help
and encouragement, I am most appreciative. I am grateful to Thomas Serfass for
preparing endless revisions and making suggestions for clarity. The many others who
have been of assistance include American Antiquarian Society, William G. Anderson
of Suffolk Community College, Robert R. Archibald of Missouri Historical Society,
Philip M. Arnold, Bank of Portugal, Francis Campbell of the ANS, John Catanzariti,
Joanne Chaison of the AAS, William Coker, Light T. Cummins, Richard Doty of the
National Museum of American History, SI, Eric P. Newman Numismatic Education
Society, Robin Fabel, Mary A. Y. Gallagher, Alan Graham of the Louisiana Archives,
John Herzog of the Museum of American Financial History, Ruth W. Hill, John N.
Hoover of St. Louis Mercantile Library, Clyde Hubbard, Kay M. Kramer, Jeremy Killie,
John M. Kleeberg of the ANS, Lancaster County Historical Society, Joseph R. Lasser,
Jose Lima, Anne S. Lipscomb of the Mississippi Department of Archives and History,
William Metcalf of the ANS, Clifford Mishler, James Mosley of St. Bride Printing
Library, Philip L. Mossman, Stan Nelson of the National Museum of American History,
Joao Candido de Lima Neto, Evelyn E. Newman, Randall Pope of Washington Univer-
sity, Jennie Rathbun and Kathleen Donovan of Harvard University Libraries, Robert
G. Sayer, Neil Shafer, Bruce W. Smith and Raymond H. Williamson.

[2] E.J. Wilber and E.P. Eastman, *A Treatise on Counterfeit, Altered, and Spurious Bank Notes* (Poughkeepsie, NY, 1865), p. 14.

[3] *American State Papers, Finance* (Washington, DC, 1832), vol. 1, p. 101.

[4] Florian Cajori, "The Evolution of the Dollar Mark," *The Popular Science Monthly* 1912, pp. 521-30.

[5] Chauncey Lee, *The American Accomptant* (Lansingburgh, NY, 1797).

[6] Florian Cajori, "More Data on the History of the Dollar Mark," *Science* 1913, p. 848; *The Numismatist* 1914, pp. 82-83.

[7] Florian Cajori in *School and Society*, vol. 21 (May 23, 1925), p. 625.

[8] Florian Cajori, "The Origin of the Dollar Mark," *The Numismatist* 1929, pp. 489-93. This information was repeated in "New Data on the Origin and Spread of the Dollar Mark," *Scientific Monthly* 1929, p. 212, and his *A History of Mathematical Notations*, vol. 2 (Chicago, 1929), pp. 15-29.

[9] Margaret F. Dalrymple, *The Merchant of Manchac: The Letterbooks of John Fitzpatrick, 1768-1790* (Baton Rouge, 1978).

[10] "Oliver Pollock Letters," *Papers of the Continental Congress*, Item 50, National Archives.

[11] James A. James, *Oliver Pollock, The Life and Times of an Unknown Patriot* (New York, 1937).

[12] Lee (above, n. 5); the printer and publisher was William W. Wands in Lansingburgh (now Troy), New York.

[13] "The Origin of the Dollar Sign," *The Numismatist* 1899, pp. 203-4.

[14] Henry L. Bullen, "Collectanea Typographica," *The Inland Printer* (Chicago, 1919), p. 645.

[15] Daniel B. Updike, *Printing Types* (Cambridge, MA, 1922).

[16] P.J. Conkwright, "Binny & Ronaldson's $ Sign," *Printing and Graphic Arts Magazine*, vol. 3 (1955), pp. 59-61.

[17] *Facts Respecting the Bank of North America* (Harrisburg and Lancaster, PA, [1799]).

[18] Daniel Adams, *The Scholar's Arithmetic or Federal Accountant* (Keene, NH, 1801).

[19] Solomon Parker's *Parker's American Citizens Sure Guide or Ready Reckoner, Measure and Calendar* (Sag Harbor, NY, 1808), p. 231, contains only a single $ sign and Samuel Webber's second edition of *Mathematics* (Cambridge, MA, 1808), uses $ signs to some extent.

[20]   Rene Paul, *Elements of Arithmetic* (St. Louis, 1823).

[21]   In addition to the works cited, the following publications have been consulted in the preparation of this study:

William G. Anderson, *The Price of Liberty* (Charlottesville, 1983).

Rafael A. Bailey, *The National Loans of the United States of America from July 4, 1776 to June 20, 1880* (Washington, 1881, 1882).

Banco de Portugal, *O Papel-Moeda em Portugal* (Lisbon, 1985).

Bank Note Reporter, Oct. 1991, p. 34.

W.H. Boozer, "The Origin of the Dollar Mark," *The Numismatist* 1931, pp. 86-87.

John D. Born, "John Fitzpatrick of Manchac," *The Journal of Mississippi History* 1970.

Q. David Bowers, *Centennial History of the American Numismatic Association*, vol. 1 (Colorado Springs, 1991), pp. 50, 91, 209, 266, 270, 421.

Stephen A. Caldwell, *A Banking History of Louisiana* (Baton Rouge, 1935).

Casa de Monedo de Mexico, *Presencia en el Mundo 1535-1990* (Mexico City, 1990), p. 43.

Henry E. Chambers, *A History of Louisiana* (Chicago, 1925).

Juan E. Cirlot, *A Dictionary of Symbols translated from Spanish*, 2nd ed. (1971).

John G. Clark, *New Orleans 1718-1812: An Economic History* (Baton Rouge, 1970).

Coin World, June 8, 1962; Oct. 11, 1978; Sept. 12, 1979; May 4, 1983.

Light T. Cummins, "Anglo Merchants and Capital Migration in Spanish Colonial New Orleans 1763-1803," *Louisiana History* (1929).

William F. De Knight, *History of the Currency of the Country and of the Loans of the United States from the Earliest Period* (Washington, DC, 1897, 1900).

"The Dollar Sign," *The Numismatist* 1928, p. 366.

"The Dollar Sign," *Rare Coin Review* 56 (1985), p. 4.

Esbozo de Una Nueva Gramatica de la Lengua Espanola (Madrid, 1983).

Robin F.A. Fabel, *The Economy of British West Florida* (Tuscaloosa, 1988).

Harwood Frost, *Evolution of the Dollar* (Chicago, 1927).

Grande Enciclopedia Portuguesa e Brasilera (Lisbon and Rio de Janeiro).

Gene Hessler, *An Illustrated History of U.S. Loans* (Port Clinton, OH, 1988).

Gene Hessler, *U.S. Essay, Proof and Specimen Notes* (Portage, OH, 1979).

James A. James, ed., *George Rogers Clark Papers 1771-1781* (Springfield, IL, 1912).

MacKellar, Smiths & Jordan, *The Printers Hand Book* (Philadelphia, 1871).

Alvaro J. Moreno, *El Signo de Pesos* (Mexico City, 1965).

"More on the Dollar Sign," *Rare Coin Review* 57 (1985), p. 51.

A New Dictionary of the Portuguese and English Languages (Leipzig, 1893).

New York Times, Dec. 8, 1912, p. 13.

Eric P. Newman, "A Numismatic Book," *The Asylum* 1988, p. 100.

Notes and Queries 1876, vol. 6, p. 386; vol. 7, p. 98.

Eduardo Nunes, "Historia portuguesa de cifrão," *Varia paleographica maiora ac minora* (Lisbon, 1973), pp. 17-27.

Numismatic News, July 16, 1991, p. 24; Aug. 13, 1991, p. 115.

O. Oddehon, "Another Theory on Origin of Dollar Sign," *Numismatic Scrapbook Magazine* 1958, p. 2345.

"The Origin of the Dollar Mark," *The Numismatist* 1909, p. 202 (quoting *The New York Times*).

"The Origin of the Dollar Mark," *The Numismatist* 1914, pp. 450-512 (quoting *The New York Independent*).

"Our Coinage," *The Numismatist* 1896, p. 165.

The Papers of Robert Morris (Pittsburgh), vol. 6 (1984); vol. 7 (1988).

The Papers of Thomas Jefferson (Princeton, 1959 et seq.).

"Queries," *The Numismatist* 1894, p. 99.

Edward C. Rochette, "The Sign of the Dollar," *The Numismatist* 1987, pp. 1659-61.

Charles N. Schmall, "Sidelights on Numismatics," *The Numismatist* 1932, p. 771.

Rollo G. Silver, *Typefounding in America, 1787-1825* (Charlottesville, 1965, 1979).

William G. Sumner, "The Spanish Dollar and the Colonial Shilling," *American Historical Review* 1898, pp. 607-19.

N. Miller Surrey, *The Commerce of Louisiana during the French Regime* (New York, 1916).

"Use of the Dollar Mark," *The Numismatist* 1896, p. 165

"What is the Origin of the Dollar Sign," *The Numismatist* 1957, p. 114.

The Early United States
Silver Dollars

Jules Reiver

Coinage of the Americas Conference
at the American Numismatic Society, New York

October 30, 1993

Striking the first United States coins was not a simple matter. Some members of the Continental Congress wanted the mark, some the eagle, and some the dollar to be our unit. In 1792 the Senate passed a bill authorizing the first coinage, and stated that George Washington should be depicted on the obverse, but the House refused to go along. When the eagle was mentioned for the reverse, one legislator commented that the eagle was the king of birds, and that we should reject anything regal. Another said, facetiously, that he agreed, and recommended using the goose, a very plebeian bird. He said that the gosling could be used on the minor coinage.

Congress finally passed the coinage bill with the weight of the dollar set at 416 grains of .8924 silver. Assayer Albion Cox found the fineness standard difficult to use. He told Director Rittenhouse that .8924 fine silver would turn black with use, whereas .900 would not. Rittenhouse accepted the argument, and the dollar contained 374.4 grains of fine silver instead of the 371.25 mandated by Congress.

On October 15, 1794, the first dollars were struck. The coining press was not designed for such a large coin, and the dies were not parallel. Many of the coins were weak on the lower obverse and corresponding reverse.

The first dollars made in 1794 and 1795 had flowing hair obverses. The reverses contained a wreath with a large eagle on it, the wings protruding through the wreath. Approximately 162,000 of this type were produced.

The next type was the draped, or fillet bust obverse with the small eagle reverse. While the other four denominations of the variety were struck only in 1796 and 1797, dollars were made in 1795, 1796, 1797 and 1798.

About 145,000 dollars were struck, but only about 112,000 of the other four denominations. While all of the flowing hair type had 15 star obverses (one for each state), the addition of Tennessee as our sixteenth state in 1796 posed a problem. It was almost impossible to cram 16 stars into the available space. Starting production with 8 stars on the left side and 7 on the right, the combination of 9 left and 7 right was used, without much success. Then, for some reason, one die was made with 10 stars on the left and 6 on the right, with even less luck. It was finally decided that only 13 stars would be used, and this standard remained for the life of the bust dollars.

There were also some changes in the reverse dies. On the large eagle varieties, some had 2 leaves and some 3 leaves under the right wing. On some small eagle reverses, small letters were used while large letters were used on others. The combinations of obverse and reverse die changes result in two types of flowing hair dollars, and six types of fillet bust, small eagle varieties.

Figure 1 depicts an odd dollar, B6.[1] Both sides are badly scratched, especially the obverse. The reverse die was heavily cracked, and one side of the coin is on a higher plane than the other. This is the only known example of the reverse, although there is a rumor that a second one exists. It is thought that the die broke on a very early strike.

1

I used this coin in a grading exercise for a youth coin class. I asked the students to grade the left side of the reverse, then the right. How can one coin have two such different grades? One of the students asked, "Mr. Reiver, do you think that the reverse die was broken on the first or second strike? If so, might the minter have thought that this broken die was too bad to be acceptable, that the die could not be used. Might he have cancelled the coin or coins, and kept one for a souvenir?" I think that it is entirely possible.

Production settled down in 1798, when the reverse was changed to the heraldic eagle with 13 stars. Approximately 1,154,000 were produced through 1803. Mint records show that 19,570 dollars were struck in 1804 and 321 in 1805. It is believed that the 1804 dollars all were dated 1803, and the 1805 coins were some that had been sent to the mint as bullion to be struck, then returned when dollars were cancelled.

Of the 90 varieties produced, only three varied from the standard. Two used the same reverse die with 15 stars, and one used an obverse die with 8 stars on the right and 5 on the left. Both of these dies were made in error.

It seems that not much silver bullion was brought to the mint to be turned into coins. Although the suppliers wanted dollars, it appears that the powers wanted to keep more people supplied with coins, and produced smaller denominations, particularly half dollars.

2

Another factor was that many of the dollars were sent out of the country, and officials preferred that the coins remain home, so no dollars were struck after 1803. A counterfeit 1805 was produced and soon became the subject of a heated argument, the owner believing it to be real.

On the subject of counterfeits, there are many. Some are cast in the Orient, mainly 1804 dollars with the AMERICAI reverse. Some castings are beautifully made like the 1794 counterfeit which fooled many collectors (fig. 2). In fact, it has ANACS papers to prove that it is authentic. There was a 1799 struck counterfeit being sold a few years ago. It was so well done that the only way to tell that it was not real was that the edge was not so nicely done.

3a   3b

3c   3d

The 1805 dollar is not the only one which we now think does not exist. Some nine varieties have been dropped by some collectors over the years. A typical case is the 12 star variety of 1798. Many years ago a *Numismatist* article described a new variety of 1798 dollar, having only 12 stars on the obverse.[2] Of course I started looking for one. When I found one, it had only 11 stars, so I continued looking. I checked the coin against all of the 1798 varieties, and found that it was B8, a common variety. Continued searching turned up one with 9 stars, one with 10, and finally, one with 12 stars (fig. 3a-d).

This led to a search for other varieties with progressive damage to the dies. Figures 4a and 4b picture the results of our latest search, die states of 1798 B28. Many of the other dies lend themselves to die state studies.

4a: early die state   4b: late die state

K.P. Austin, who bought the entire Bolender collection, offered me an unlisted 1795 variety, for a very high price. I checked it, and decided that it was merely a die state. I took color slides to prove my point, and drove to Louisiana to argue with Frank Stirling, a true dollar specialist, who had told me that the new variety was valid. I set up the projector and started to show slides. When Frank saw what I was about, he said, "Shucks, Jules, I was just pulling your leg. Emanuel Taylor told me that it was a die state in 1926."

Also of interest to collectors are error coins. There are many examples which have been struck two or more times. You will hear talks on counterstamped and engraved dollars, and plugged centers. Another category is engraver's errors. Figure 5 depicts one where the date was punched in as 1195, instead of 1795. On the scarce 1797 B2 variety, a star was punched far below the star left of L on the obverse. On the 1795 B13 the B in LIBERTY was punched in

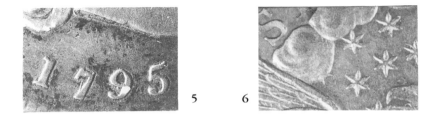

5   6

twice. The diesinker then punched an E over the second B. My favorite one is the reverse die used on 1799 B3 and B4. The engraver mistakenly punched 15 stars on the reverse, realized his mistake, and tried to pull the two end clouds down to cover two of the stars (fig. 6).

All in all, this is a very interesting series to collect.

---

[1]   References are to M.H. Bolender, *The United States Early Silver Dollars from 1794 to 1803*, 5th ed. (Iola, WI, 1988).

[2]   H.N. Shepherd, "New Variety 1798 Silver Dollar?" *The Numismatist* 1966, pp. 571-72.

1795 United States Silver Dollar with Official Plug

Kenneth Bressett

**Coinage of the Americas Conference
at the American Numismatic Society, New York**

October 30, 1993

Several years ago I became intrigued by some unusual silver dollars that I had seen (fig. 1). They were all dated 1795, and had a curious circular ring or seam showing at the center on each side. The imperfection looked like a carefully repaired hole that had been plugged with silver and then disguised to hide the work. There had to be a reason for so many coins showing the same peculiarity, so I resolved to find the answer.

1

After examining several of these coins I found that the flaw was not simply a repair, but in fact was something that had been done at the Mint before the coins were struck. Evidence of this was clear because there could be no doubt that the design impressed from the dies was on top of the spot in question. There had been no tooling or other repair to the area after the coins had been struck.

The unusual dollars with this curious feature are all dated 1795. They look just like other dollars of the period except for a telltale circle which can be seen at the center on each side. The detail can best be described as a silver plug which has been imbedded in the planchet before normal striking. In some cases only a seam, or discoloration at the coin's center, shows on one or both sides.

Just why plugs were added to these coins is a mystery. Most of the silver dollars of 1795 do not have a plug, and no dollars of any other date have this same feature. Indeed, as far as I know, no other coin denomination in the regular United States series was officially altered with a plug of any kind.

There is, however, precedent for a comparable plug. A similar circumstance occurred with the 1792 "silver center" pattern pieces. Those coins were made with a silver dowel inserted in the center of a copper planchet prior to striking. The reason for that experiment was to raise the intrinsic value of the copper to full face value. No such effort would have been necessary in the case of the 1795 dollars because the entire coin was made of silver and adding a plug would not change the value in any way.

It is curious that no information has ever before been published about these unusual coins. Perhaps they were simply not noticed in the past. A few numismatists have known about them for a decade, but no one has attempted to explain the strange alteration. It is reasonable to believe that many specimens have been overlooked because of the subtle difference in their appearance. Perhaps that will change now that they have been separately catalogued in print.[1]

The number of pieces originally produced at the Mint with these plugs can be estimated only roughly. I believe it must have been substantial based on the availability of surviving specimens and the number of die combinations involved in making the coins. In searching for specimens in dealers' stocks, I was able to identify a dozen pieces in a six-month period. Apparently they are still relatively prevalent, and the original mintage must have been quite extensive.

All of the 1795 plugged dollars seen so far are of the Flowing Hair type. No 1795 Draped Bust pieces with this feature have been noted. The varieties examined are Bolender number 1, 3, 4, 7, and 9.[2] In every case many more "normal" specimens are known of each of these varieties. Continued search has failed to turn up any additional varieties, but many more of the plugged coins have been reported since publication of information about them.

In each case, the plugs were inserted before the coins were struck. The insert has been impacted by dies, and carries impressions of the obverse and reverse designs. The plugs average about 8 mm in diameter and usually are evident on both sides of the coin. They are always located at the approximate center of the specimen.

Q. David Bowers suggests that the striking sequence of 1795 dollars indicates that the known varieties of plugged coins were made early in the series. According to his research, they must have been made near late summer of 1795.[3] The entire production apparently took place around the middle of the year, and before any of the Draped Bust dollars were coined. The dollars of 1794 have been so carefully studied it seems improbable that any of them were plugged and have gone unnoticed. It also seems likely that no plugged pieces were made later than 1795.

A student of early coinage, Roger Burdette, also puzzled over the strange plugged dollars for some time and concluded that the insert was done at the Mint to adjust either the weight, or the silver content of the planchet. We found that each of us had the same suspicion, and concluded that the most reasonable premise was that the plug was intended to correct an error in the fineness of the metal. The question was, why would only some of the 1795 dollars show this unique form of planchet adjustment, when no other coin in the entire U.S. series has been so treated.

There was good reason to suspect that planchets for the 1795 dollars needed to be adjusted to bring them to the correct fineness for silver as authorized by Congress. It is a matter of record that some of the early United States coins were not made correctly. The oversight occurred when Mint Director David Rittenhouse took it upon himself to allow coins to be made of an illegal standard to reconcile the strange .89243 thousandths fineness mandated by Congress. He reasoned that the standard was flawed in specifying a complicated fineness of 1485/1664th, at a time when their technology did not permit accurate verification.

It seemed likely that Director Rittenhouse, who sought to change the standard, was encouraged by the supporting report of a committee of the House. Relying on his more practical approach, he decided to use an alloy of .900 fine silver. This produced a coin with 374.75 grains of silver and a total weight of 416.39 grains. Both Thomas Jefferson and Alexander Hamilton thought this an acceptable solution, and Rittenhouse produced many dollars during 1795 using the unauthorized alloy.

Unfortunately, his alteration had the effect of adding a small amount to the value of the silver in each coin; and eventually Rittenhouse was caught by a depositor of bullion who argued that he did not receive the full number of dollars for the amount of silver he had turned over to the Mint. John Vaughn, who noticed this discrepancy, charged that by adding about 3.5 grains of extra silver to each dollar, the Mint had cheated him out of $2,620. He demanded reimbursement from Congress, and his claim was approved in February of 1800.

This scenario speaks well for the possibility of the strange plugged dollars being part of a maneuver by Rittenhouse to correct the fineness of planchets that had been prepared to the illegal standard. As tempting as this conclusion is to ponder, it is flawed, and does not seem to be the actual reason for the alteration. The use of multiple dies to strike the plugged pieces indicates a practice that went on over a period of time, and would negate the theory of a wholesale repair of sub-standard planchets.

A simpler and more plausible explanation is that the plug was used to adjust the weight of these coins. Planchet preparation in those days was costly and time consuming. Any that were too heavy could be filed to remove excess metal, but underweight planchets had to be melted and remade. Many examples of early U.S. coins are known showing adjustment marks made by filing the planchets before striking. Until now, nothing has been known about how underweight planchets might have been corrected.

The answer seems to be that the during mid-1795 an experiment was tried in the mint to salvage lightweight planchets by inserting a dowel, or plug, in the center of the piece and then striking it with normal dies. There would be no need to drill a hole, or remove any metal. A simple piercing with a sharp instrument would leave an opening where a pin or dowel could be inserted. The effect after striking would be to round over the exposed tips on each side of the coin, much like the ends of rivet used in building construction.

Further proof of this hypothesis was derived from tests I conducted on several pieces to ascertain the metal content of both the coin and plug. If plugs were added to adjust the fineness, they would be of lower fineness than the coin itself, which, according to Rittenhouse, exceeded the fineness specified by law. If, on the other hand, the plugs were added to adjust the weight, their fineness would be similar to the rest of the coin.

In most cases where tests were made, spectrographic X-ray analysis showed that both the plug and the coin were made of the same alloy. With one specimen, the plug was of higher fineness; a second specimen contained a plug of lower fineness. For others there was little or no difference.

Although these tests do not establish the exact nature and reason for the plugs being inserted into these coins, it seems safe to conclude that the plugs were added to bring the underweight planchets up to standard. Why this practice involved only silver dollar blanks, and only Flowing Hair pieces of 1795 is puzzling. One possibility is that it was part of an effort to produce a large quantity of dollar blanks to be stored and ready for production when a new more powerful coinage press would be ready for operation.

On May 6, 1795, that press was put in use, and thousands of dollars were delivered shortly thereafter. Surely some or all of them were made from the old stockpile of planchets, which could have included an indiscriminate number of blanks that had been adjusted by plugging. Drawing planchets from such a storehouse would account for the arbitrary use of plugged blanks mixed with normal planchets, and they would have been used in the production of coins from several die combinations.

Further evidence of this extraordinary method of weight adjustment has been discovered by Horace P. Flatt in a documented account of how coins were produced in Lima, Peru, about the same time.[4] The pertinent part reads as follows:

...The next process is the weighing; the person who per-
forms this has a little square box containing silver pins
that are no longer than the thickness of a dollar, and of
different weights and sizes; the dollars are thrown one
by one into the scales, but seldom any of them are too
heavy, when they are, they generally pass them without
notice, but if any are too light a pin is thrown into the
scale which brings it to the standard weight.

The dollar is then put under a screw which has a
pointed instrument in the end of it, which is screwed
down and pierces a hole in the dollar sufficiently large
to receive the pin; then it is placed under another screw
with a smooth end, which completely fastens the pin in
the coin; they are then passed into another room where
they are coined.

This description seems to fit exactly the manufacturing process
necessary to produce the effect seen on these 1795 dollars. It would
be an effective and accurate method of adding to the weight of the
planchets. Once coined the corrected pieces would hardly be discer-
nible. In fact one specimen recently examined by Bowers and still
in choice Uncirculated condition, showed the plug clearly only on
the obverse side.[5] It seems likely that with wear, many of these
repaired pieces would go undetected until toning or close scrutiny
revealed a faint trace of something unnatural.

Indeed, most of these curious pieces have gone unnoticed until
recent times. Perhaps now that they are better known we will be
able to learn more about them. Or perhaps additional coins of other
denominations or dates will be found. It is a challenge well worth
pursuing to help better understand the intriguing and little known
history of minting practices in the early U.S. Mint.

[1]   R.S. Yeoman, *Guide Book of United States Coins*, 47th ed. (Racine, WI, 1993),
pp. 170-71; Q. David Bowers, *Silver Dollars and Trade Dollars of the United States*
(Wolfeboro, NH, 1993), pp. 185ff.

[2]   M.H. Bolender, *The United States Early Silver Dollars from 1794 to 1803*, 5th
ed. (Iola, WI, 1988).

[3]   Bowers (above, n. 1), pp. 186-87.

[4]   Amassa Delano, *Narrative of Voyages and Travels in the Northern and Southern
Hemispheres* (Boston, 1817).

[5]   Q. David Bowers, 1993. Personal correspondence with the author.

Countermarked and Overstruck
Early U. S. Dollars

Robert Stark

Coinage of the Americas Conference
at the American Numismatic Society, New York

October 30, 1993

"Those of us who have wandered down the numismatic byroad that leads to the study of countermarks occasionally find ourselves far from the beaten path, bogged down in a quagmire of uncertainty. Fanciful conjecture sometimes influences our attempts to decipher some obscure hieroglyphic impressed upon a coin by an individual in some perilous time past."[1]

So wrote Edward Fisher in a recent article dealing with nineteenth century Mexican countermarks; and it somewhat applies here. About two years ago, I saw a few countermarks on early dollars, and made a note of them. As a student of our early dollars, my interest had less to do with countermarks than with the usage of our early dollars. Several dozen countermarks have come to my attention since—and for some there is a history of sorts—but for the most part they pose questions to which answers are yet to be evident.

As information accumulates one classifies. These four classifications of countermarks and overstrikes have been useful: a) personal pocket pieces; b) merchant advertising; c) to certify value; and d) to endorse local use.

Personal Pocket Pieces

Many of the countermarked early dollars bear initials. This difficult group probably comprises the personal pocket pieces.

A 1799 dollar with initials FW and 1863 in script and a less fancy B and C is an example. Could it have been carried by a Union soldier? And if it was ..., well, you can imagine the questions we might have; especially since by 1863, a 1799 dollar was a "keeper."

Countermarked names provide better prospects for identification, but certainly not in every instance. W.B. Joy is countermarked on a 1798 dollar. Who was W.B. Joy? M. Miner also appears on a 1798 dollar. As yet, no clue to an identity. If these people were merchants or otherwise prominent, it is likely that they will eventually be identified because of the microfilm availability of earlier newspapers and city directories.

L.L. Squire on a 1795 dollar is probably the work of L. L. Squire and Sons, ship chandlers and rope makers on Front Street in New York (fig. 1). Besides rope and candles the firm dealt in oils, paints, anchors, chain cables, and naval stores.

C.C. Clark (Carlos C. Clark), appears on a 1799 and an 1802 dollar. Clark, a New England gunsmith, seems to have had a penchant for recording dates on early dollars, which could record significant dates in his career. On the 1802 dollar there are three dates: 1842, 1864, 1879, and an engraved flower. Russell Rulau conjectures that he began self-employment in Windsor, VT, as a gunsmith in 1842.[2]

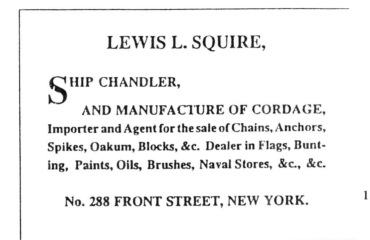

LEWIS L. SQUIRE,

S HIP CHANDLER,

AND MANUFACTURE OF CORDAGE,

Importer and Agent for the sale of Chains, Anchors, Spikes, Oakum, Blocks, &c. Dealer in Flags, Bunting, Paints, Oils, Brushes, Naval Stores, &c., &c.

No. 288 FRONT STREET, NEW YORK. 1

There are records that he was employed from 1846 to 1856 by percussion riflemakers Robbins and Lawrence. He moved to New Hampshire about 1863 and possibly the 1864 date on the coin refers to the actual date of relocation. The 1879 date may indicate retirement. A 1799 dollar, apparently using the same or similar punches, bears his name and the dates 1842 to 1879.

Abram Brinsmaid, a Burlington, VT silversmith, was born in Great Barrington, MA, in 1770, and died in Burlington in 1811. His firm and its successors, Brinsmaid and Hildreth, used his hallmark years after his death. The same hallmark is known on silverware in addition to this double struck 1795 flowing hair dollar (fig. 2). This dollar

2

is prominently double struck and it is a very rare die variety (Bolender 8) of which only a few are known. Since the mint delivered coins in exchange for a corresponding weight of precious metal, possibly the production of this rare variety went to the Burlington area.

An H.G. Stone hallmark on an 1803 dollar is attributed to Hubbard Stone, a New York silversmith (fig. 3).

3

"EB counterstamp, fodder for legends," is the lead line for a *Coin World* article by William Swoger.[3] These are the doubloon and the George III Guinea. They represent Ephraim Brasher's trade of certifying foreign gold coins for use locally. The New York goldsmith lived from 1744-1810 (and counted George Washington among his circle). Note that as initialed coins these fit a personal piece category. As a known hallmark they fit the advertising category; and as assays they fit the certification for value and even the authorization for local use categories. So much for any attempts at unambiguous classification.

The fame of the EB countermark tempts some to attribute all of them to Brasher. Milfred Bolender, whose early dollar book has been a valuable standard for many years (although it is now inadequate), attributes a 1799 dollar with an EB countermark to Brasher.[4] But some point out that Brasher may have only countermarked gold coins. Gregory Brunk, a foremost student of countermarks, asserts that not all the EB countermarks seen on coins belong to Brasher. He suggests that this one in particular may belong to Ezekiel Burr, a Providence silversmith who died in 1846.[5]

Prepared solely from Vegetable Matter,

By JACOB HOUCK, Baltimore,

Which may be taken with perfect safety by all ages and in all diseases; Its cures are for the following diseases—Dyspepsia, Loss of Appetite, Indigestion, Inflamation of the Stomach, Heart Burn, Diarrhea, Dysentary or Flux, Piles, Fistula, Obstructed Menstruation, Ague and Fever, Billious or Remittent Fever, Typus Fever, Scarlet Fever, Small Pox, Erysipelous of St. Anthony's Fire, Asthma, Pleurisy, Measels, Yellow Fever, Costiveness, Wind on the Stomach or Bowels, Cholera Morbus; Consumption, Influenza, Colds, Coughs, Inflammation of the chest, Palsey, Gout, Rheumatism, Inflammatory Sore Throat or Quinsey, Whooping Cough, Thrush or Sore Mouth, Putrid Sore Throat, Croup, Inflammation of the Heart, Dropsy, Rickets, Diseases of the Liver, Jaundice, Difficulty of making Urine, Gleet, Histerics, Nervous & Scrofulous Affections of the Members and Ligaments, Mercurial and Venereal Diseases, Ulcers, Sores, Affections of the Skin, and all diseases arising from Impure Blood, &c.

Price per Bottle $1 50.

The above medicine can be obtained at No. 121 Market street, opposite the Museum, with proper directions for using. A liberal discount made to persons who buy to sell.

5

But, is it Ezekiel Burr? An authoritative volume by Belden on early American silver lists and attributes EB hallmarks to various silversmiths.[6] A bit of detective work probably can settle this.

L. Bailey on a 1795 bust dollar has been attributed Lebbus Bailey, a Portland, ME gunsmith although Q. David Bowers thinks Loring Bailey, a Hingham (or Hull), MA silversmith is a better answer.[7] His thought is prompted by the hallmark—it was more likely to be used by a silversmith than a gunsmith. The piece supports a conjecture that a coin could be handy piece on which to try a new punch or puncher. It follows that writing off all EBs not on gold as not belonging to Brasher may be hasty.

Merchant Advertising

Finally, among the merchants, is the popular favorite, Houck's Panacea, which appears on a 1795 dollar in the SI and on an 1883 half dollar in the ANS (fig. 4). An ad from an early Baltimore City Directory (fig. 5), suggests that today, some 150 years later, medical science still seeks Houck's Panacea.

The countermarking by silversmiths seems to be a practice of those in the northeast. I don't know of silversmiths south of New York (and most are from New England), who countermarked early dollars.

4

Certify Value

British merchants certified value in local currency. The splendid mark of the Scottish Copper and Coal Co. of John Wilson appears on an 1800 dollar in the ANS, the gift of Mrs. R. Henry Norweb in

1967 (fig. 6). Note the 5 shilling value and the Scottish town of Hurlet.

Two other Scottish merchant countermarks are known. One belongs to John McLean on a 1799 dollar with inscribed value 5 shillings, 3 pence and the Scottish town of Paisley. The third such is countermarked "WG and Co" and 4 shillings, 9 pence.

That these three merchant countermarks originated in Scotland, probably as a response to the severe British coin shortage about that time, suggests that the officially counterstamped George III pieces didn't reach the Scots in adequate quantities.

In the last years of the eighteenth century and into the early 1800s, Britain experienced a severe shortage of circulating silver. The British possessed sizable quantities of captured Spanish dollars and in an attempt to relieve the shortage, the king's head, used to mark silver, was stamped on the head of the Spanish king, Charles IV, in March 1797. These were to be valued at 4 shillings and 6 pence each. However, before issue it was discovered that the bullion value was 4 and 8; a melt value of two pence higher than the intended face value. Simple solution: to prevent melting, revalue them at 4 and 9. About 2 million were issued according to Howland Wood, an early student of the subject.[8] The issue was immediately counterfeited which seems to give credence to a couplet of the time, "The Bank to make the Spanish dollar pass, stamped the head of a fool on the head of an ass." The issue was demonetized in May 1804. It was then announced that Mr. Boulton of Soho Mint fame had been engaged to produce a new dollar by obliterating the Spanish markings. A 5 shilling dollar, Bank of England, 1804, with a George III obverse, and a Bank of Ireland 6 shilling dollar are in the ANS.

The relevance of this to early dollars is that while the official Act applied only to the Spanish dollars, an oval George III countermark appears on a 1795 flowing hair dollar and octagonal impressions (intended to make counterfeiting more difficult) are known on 1798 and 1799 dollars. What is not known is whether these royal countermarks on U.S. dollars are counterfeits, possibly intended to aid foreign coinage to pass more readily. An early Bangs catalogue shows the royal countermark on a U.S. 1795 half dollar.[9] Modern fakes are uninteresting; but counterfeits of the time were, after all, circulating coinage.

Endorse Local Use

Much U.S. coinage circulated or was melted south of our border. Indeed, some believe that President Thomas Jefferson halted dollar production at least in part because of such melting.

An "R.F. 1845" countermark has appeared on several dates including an 1800 dollar. It has been suggested that these could have been made for the French Caribbean, say Guadeloupe; the R.F. standing for "République Français." Brunk is adamant that these are fantasy pieces that never saw the Caribbean.[10]

It is possible that some of the support for Caribbean usage came from a French edict of 1802 for Guadeloupe that silver-dollar sized coins have octagonal sections cut from the center and stamped "4E" (for the local currency) and "R.F." (fig. 7).[11] Again, one can't say that this isn't a fantasy piece.

7

8

A holed 1800 dollar with a "fleur de lis" counterstamp in the ANS (fig. 8) is housed in a box containing a note to the effect that it was counterstamped by decree of the Governor General on November 27, 1884, and "the collectors of customs at Fajardo, Guayama, Ponce, Mayaguez, Arecibo, Vieques and San Juan counterstamped them to validate the holed coins then in circulation." It is a late date for a circulating early dollar!

Further south in Uruguay, during a nine-year siege of Montevideo (1843-1852), pesos were struck on our early dollars. Two examples are known. One is on a 1799 dollar recently sold by Superior Galleries[12] and the other on a 1798 dollar in the ANS (fig. 9).

9

Finally, I note two unusual 1794 dollars. The first is a 1794 dollar countermarked "F7" for Ferdinand VII, apparently for use in the Philippines, then under Spanish rule.[13] A note in a later issue of *The Numismatist* indicates that the coin was among other loot offered for sale in California.[14] Its current whereabouts are unknown to me.

The second, a 1795 dollar (Bolender 4), struck over a 1794 dollar belongs to Bowers and Merena Galleries, Inc. The obverse clearly shows the outline of the eagle, wreath and parts of United. The reverse shows some profile and back of Liberty's head. The coin was discovered by Breen who speculated on its origins.[15] I have some recollection that he once entertained the idea that the mint may have struck a round number of 1794 dollars, say 2,000 pieces. The reported mintage of 1,758 pieces, nearly none of high quality, may be all that were judged even marginally useful as coinage. This piece, struck so weakly, may have kept it from the melting pot to await a proper coin press the next year.

[1]   Edward S. Fisher, "A New Twist on an Old Countermark," *The Numismatist* 1993, p. 1239.

[2]   Russell Rulau, *U.S. Merchant Tokens, 1845–1860* (Iola, 1990), p. 75.

[3]   *CW* June 1, 1992.

[4]   M.H. Bolender, *The United States Early Silver Dollars from 1794 to 1803* 5th ed. (Iola, WI, 1988), p. 55 (B-8a).

[5]   Gregory C. Brunk, *American and Canadian Countermarked Coins* (Rockford, IL, 1987), p. 66.

[6]   Louise C. Belden, *Marks of American Silversmiths in the Ineson-Bissel Collection* (Charlottesville, 1980).

[7]   Bowers and Merena, Nov. 18-19, 1993, 3114.

[8]   Howland Wood, "The Bank of England Counterstamp on United States Money," *The Numismatist* 1904, p. 358.

[9]   William E. Woodward, May 21-25, 1888 ("Vicksburg Cabinet" [George M. Klein]), 1947.

[10]   Brunk (above, n. 5), p. 145.

[11]   Howland Wood, "The Coinage of the West Indies with Especial Reference to the Cut and Counterstamped Pieces," *AJN* 48 (1914), p. 100.

[12]   Superior Galleries, Sept. 26-28, 1993, 856 and see *CW* Sept. 20, 1993 and Nov. 15, 1993.

[13]   P.I. de Jesus, "Early Coins of the Philippines," *The Numismatist* 1947, pp. 270, 272 (I owe this reference to John Kleeberg).

[14]   "Looted Coins Being Offered," *The Numismatist* 1949, p. 366.

[15]   Cited in Q. David Bowers, *Silver Dollars and Trade Dollars of the United States. A Complete Encyclopedia* (Wolfeboro, NH, 1993), p. 199.

The Development of the
1878 Morgan Silver Dollars

A. George Mallis

**Coinage of the Americas Conference
at the American Numismatic Society, New York**

October 30, 1993

Background

The Morgan silver dollar, originally known as the Bland silver dollar after its sponsor in Congress, was designed by an Englishman, George T. Morgan.[1] The unusual set of circumstances which led to Morgan, rather than having the dollar designed in the normal procedure by the then mint chief engraver, William Barber, or his assistants, can partially be explained in the letters between Linderman and Fremantle, the Deputy Director of the Royal Mint in London.

Dr. Henry Richard Linderman, Director of the Mint, was responsible for this change in the procedure for the designing of U.S. coins. In 1876, Linderman wanted to change the silver coinage designs and felt that additional engravers were needed. On June 13, 1876, he sent a letter to C.W. Fremantle, Deputy Master, Royal Mint, London, asking Fremantle "to find a first class die-sinker who would be willing to take the position of assistant engraver at the Mint at Philadelphia."

Further in the letter, Linderman went on to say that (and this is vital to the issue):

> The engraving of coinage and medal dies has not been brought to much perfection in this country. In England it appears to have reached a standard equal, if not superior, to that of any other country.[2]

Fremantle replied to Linderman in a letter of July 31, 1876:

> My inquiries as to an Assistant Engraver lead me very strongly to recommend for the post Mr. George Morgan, age 30, who has made himself a considerable name, but for whom there is not much opening at present in this country.

Fremantle further noted in this letter:

> I have lost no time in taking steps to obtain for you designs in this country for the head of "Liberty" to be put upon your silver coin...I put myself in communication with Messrs. J.S. and A.B. Wyon, Mr. Leonard Wyon (Engravers of the Mint)....

A further letter on September 19, 1876 from Fremantle to Linderman mentioned sending:

> Those designs in plaster of the head of Liberty for the obverse of your silver coinage...you will have already received the designs sent by Messrs. J.S. and A.B. Wyon.

From this letter it is evident that Linderman was at that time obtaining sample LIBERTY HEAD designs for use on U.S. coins from the Mint in England. It may also indicate that Linderman was not entirely satisfied with Barber's work and might have influenced him later in his choice of designers for the new silver dollar proposed under the Bland-Allison Act.

Morgan agreed to work at the Philadelphia Mint for a trial six-month appointment reporting directly to Linderman, followed by a longer period if things worked out.[3] Morgan was 31 when he left Liverpool, England, on September 27, 1876, on the steamship *Illinois*,[4] and arrived in Philadelphia on October 9, 1876. He served at the Philadelphia Mint as an Assistant Engraver under William Barber, later serving in the same capacity under William Barber's son until 1917, when he was appointed chief engraver. Morgan held this office until his death on January 4, 1925, at the age of 79.

Morgan's Initial Work[5]

Morgan did not begin work on the silver dollar until a year after he arrived at the Philadelphia Mint. His first year's work, however, laid the foundation for the design of the silver dollar, since a number of pattern dies were made with devices similar to that of the silver dollar. His first designs were for pattern half dollar pieces.

After arriving in the United States Morgan stayed at Mrs. Eckfeldt's boarding house at 1614 Mount Vernon Street in Philadelphia.[6] He did his initial modeling work there since at the Mint, according to Barber, there was not sufficient space. In an August 16, 1878 letter from Pollock, Superintendent of the Philadelphia Mint to Linderman, Barber mentioned that:

> Space and Light in our Engraver's office are limited. I would be at a loss to know where to put Mr. Morgan that he could work to advantage.

William T. Barber, Chief Engraver, and his assistant and son, Charles E. Barber, were probably not very cooperative with George Morgan since he was an outsider who had the special privilege of reporting directly to Dr. Linderman. Thus, Morgan was forced not only to develop his designs in the less than ideal place of his residence but also to endure the hostile atmosphere of the Mint Engraving Department.

On November 1, 1876, Morgan took his first model of a reverse eagle to the Mint for reduction. During November and December 1876, Morgan presented additional models of the reverse eagle and obverse Liberty head for the half dollar. In Morgan's letter of January 8, 1877, to Linderman, he forwarded wax impressions of three dies to Linderman for his criticism. The letter stated:

No. 1 An impression from a wax mold taken from the
working hub...and also shows the uneven surfaces where
I have cut down the ground and round the body of the
eagle....

(Apparently there is no pattern available showing that eagle design.)
No. 2: is the same design with a different treatment of
the wings - I have yet another in hand where I make the
feathers of the wings as large as No. 1, but to radiate from
a center as in No. 2.

(These eagles are shown in Judd Patterns 1514 and 1516, showing
an eagle with out-stretched but stubby wings and encircled with a
ring of pearls.)[7]
In No. 3 you will notice that the outline of the face is
too bold. I have the profile eagle so far advanced that I
hope to be able to send you an impression this day week.
The other head is being electroplated previous to reduction by the machine.

(No. 3 impression mentioned in Morgan's letter was the obverse
Liberty head shown in Judd 1514 and 1516 similar to that used on
the Morgan dollar but encircled with a ring of pearls. The profile
eagle also is encircled with a ring of pearls that was ready a week
later and is shown in Judd 1512.) Specimen coins from these dies
were struck and forwarded to Linderman early in February 1877.

These first half dollar specimens all had the same Liberty head
design on the obverse with identical other design features of stars,
ring of pearls and denticles. The reverse had three different eagles
with a large scroll beneath the eagle that was the same except for
size. All have the same ring of pearls of 121 dots surrounding the
center designs on both sides and all have the same outer ring of 120
small denticles on both sides. So there are common design elements
in all three specimens. Morgan seemed to prefer working with three
design combinations as this number repeats time and again
throughout his design refinement work.

These original designs included the Liberty heads, eagles and
wreathes but not the peripheral lettering, stars and dates. The dies
and hubs were destroyed at the Philadelphia mint on May 25, 1910.
Clearly, many different dies and hubs of Liberty heads, eagles and
wreaths were prepared by Morgan and William Barber during the
1876-78 time period.

Although the dies and hubs made by Morgan were all destroyed
in 1910, the Philadelphia Mint still has a number of Galvanos of
Morgan designs. These include an eagle clutching a scroll, olive
branch and arrows similar to Judd 1516, an eagle with outstretch-

ed wing similar to the $10 gold pattern and initial dollar pattern, and the $10 gold obverse pattern.[8] None of the Galvanos have lettering or stars around the edges but show only the central design.

Initial Design of the Silver Dollars

The Act of Congress which proposed the coinage of silver dollars stated that there should appear on the silver dollar the devices and superscriptions provided by the Act of January 18, 1837, Section 13. Six silver pattern dollars, bearing the designs of both Morgan and Barber, were forwarded to Linderman on December 5, 1877 (figs. 1-2).[9] In a letter regarding these pattern dollars, coiner O.C. Bosbyshell wrote to Superintendent Pollock:

> I also send one of the latter's (Barber's) designs in copper, in order to show clearly the work on his dies, as the silver are not as satisfactorily brought up as could have been desired.

1. Pattern silver dollar by Morgan.

2. Pattern silver dollar by Barber.

This trouble with Barber's design was to have an important bearing on Linderman's eventual choice of the design to be used. It should be noted that the old English letters used for the motto "In God We Trust" of Morgan's dollar was to make it the only U.S. coin to have old English letters in its composition and to use both upper and lower case letters. It was also at that time the only U.S. coin to have an engraver's initial (M) on both the obverse and reverse. Morgan experienced some problems with these pattern dies during the striking of additional pattern pieces in December 1877.

Morgan was also carrying out the first of many alterations of the silver dollar design. His letter to Linderman on January 30 details these alterations:

> I have the working hubs for the silver dollar now finished. While making these hubs I have taken care to reduce the relief in places where from the specimens already made I found it necessary. I have also altered the eagle cutting away the wings from the legs and making a few other minor alterations...I understand that it was your desire that I should see Col. Snowden I found his criticism very valuable and have adopted his suggestions almost entirely.

Colonel A. Loudon Snowden was, thus, the third person beside Morgan who influenced the design of the silver dollar.[10] Linderman was concerned with the progress of these alterations and wrote Pollock January 29, February 7, and again on February 9, requesting that new specimens be forwarded to him when they were struck. In mid-February, Linderman made a visit to the Philadelphia mint and instructed Morgan:

> To make some slight modifications in the reverse die engraved by him for the silver dollar.

Pete Bishal of Fall River, MA, has studied the denticles of the Morgan patterns and regular issue dies and has pointed out that the original dollar patterns had 151 denticles on the obverse and reverse and that later pattern reverses still had 151 denticles whereas later pattern reverses had 148 denticles.

Other Morgan pattern dollars exist showing additional minor design refinements. These are changes suggested by Col. Snowden or requested by Linderman during January and February 1878. None quite match the working dies that were eventually used in the regular coinage, however (fig. 3).

In a letter to Pollock on February 21, 1878, Linderman inquired when the modifications by Morgan would be completed so that a specimen could be forwarded to his office. He also added:

3. (Wings cut down).

I have now to state for your information, that it is my intention, in the event of the silver bill now pending in Congress becoming law, to request the approval by the Secretary of the Treasury of the dies prepared by Mr. Morgan.

It is the desire of the Secretary of the Treasury, as well as my own, that if the silver bill becomes law, the coinage of silver dollars shall be commenced with the least practicable delay and carried to the full capacity of the mints for the execution of such coinage. It is proper to add that the specimens struck from the dies prepared by Messrs. Morgan and Barber exhibit high skill as well as artistic taste and that there is little if any difference in their matters, but that since a choice has to be made, I have selected the one having the lowest relief and requiring the lightest power to bring up the devices and inscriptions. No mention, however, of my preference need be made until after the receipt of the specimens herein called for and notification to you of its adoption.

Thus, Linderman preferred the Morgan design over Barber's design because of its lower design relief and desired the least delay in commencing the silver dollar coinage once the silver bill became law.

Morgan wrote to Linderman on February 22, that the dies with alterations would be ready in a few days. He added some comments on the process of making these dies:

I made the alterations on the working hub, which was hardened on Monday last...

These alterations make the working hub for the reverse useless as a regular working hub. I can make a specimen die from it, by cutting a part of the work in the die.

It is clear from this letter and Morgan's letter of January 30, that alterations were made by cutting away the working hub, thus reducing the size and relief of the design. He could have also added and strengthened details by cutting into the master die. But for major changes, Morgan may have gone back to the design die or hub in order to make a new master die. This may have happened for the reverse in February 1878, when the eagle's tail feathers were changed from seven to eight and the number of olive leaves at the end of the branch was changed from three to nine. Production of the working dies was a slow process requiring from seven to ten blows of the working hub at the rate of one blow a day. This fact will later prove important.

Both of the reverse working hubs mentioned in the above letter were eventually used to make working dies that struck coins. As will be shown later, this caused two minor design types of the 8 tail feather reverse. Soon afterward, Morgan visited Colonel Snowden for his opinion about the alterations.

On February 28, the day that Congress passed the Bland-Allison silver dollar bill, Linderman wrote to Pollock ordering that the alterations be made to the working hub:

> You will instruct Mr. Morgan to finish his new working hubs, showing the alterations, as speedily as may be practicable, and that immediately thereafter you will cause working dies to be made in sufficient quantity to commence striking pieces as soon as possible after the bill may become a law...

On March 1, Linderman sent the following telegram to Pollock:

> The specimen sent on twenty fifth ulto Morgan modified die has been approved and adopted. Conform strictly to it in making new working hubs.

In a separate telegram the same day, he ordered:

> Commence at once the preparation of silver dollar blanks to your full capacity and get the working dies ready as soon as possible and commence striking. The full force of the Engravers Department will be applied to the preparation of silver dollar dies.

The Philadelphia mint was, therefore, under great pressure to begin striking the new silver dollar.

President Hayes and Secretary of the Treasury John Sherman had expressed to Linderman a desire to possess the first and second specimens, respectively, of the regular silver dollar coinage. In a letter to Pollock on February 28, Linderman ordered:

> You will instruct the coiner to hand you the first piece

struck and the second piece, with a certificate of their
being the first and second pieces struck and transmit the
certificates to me.

So ended the initial design changes of the 1878 Morgan silver
dollar but, unfortunately, not its troubles.

Design Changes in the Regular Coinage

The first coins were not struck until two weeks after the law was
passed. The initial delivery of 303 coins was sent to Linderman on
March 12. The first three coins went to President Hayes, Secretary
of the Treasury John Sherman, and Mint Director Linderman. Con-
temporary newspaper accounts indicate that the first dollar struck
in the presses used for regular coinage of the new silver dollar was
struck at 3:17 in the afternoon of March 11, 1878, at the Philadelphia
mint.

The first dollar struck for regular issue, given to President Hayes,
now resides in the Rutherford B. Hayes Museum at Fremont, Ohio,
and is a VAM 9.[11]

4. I Obv.   5. A Rev.

The first obverse design exists in I[1] and I[2] minor design types
(fig. 4). The I[1] has an incused (recessed) designer's initial "M". The
I[2] has a raised (cameo) designer's initial, "M", with two parallel
vertical bars.

There are two different A design reverse hubs with minor design
differences (fig. 5). The A1 reverse has a raised eagle's beak and the
A2 reverse has a hooked eagle's beak.

The high relief of the eight tail feather design shortened the life
of the dies. In order to make the dies produce better, "efforts of
ingenuity" were used as Barber put it in a letter to Pollock on March
23:

> I wish to report that by using what I might call "efforts
> of ingenuity" we have succeeded in making our dies pro-
> duce "very well" this last five days...

Unfortunately, the details of these irregular methods were not given
in this letter. Examination of the die varieties of the first reverse
design (8 TF) indicates that some working dies were individually
reengraved, adding two to three small feathers to both sides of the
eagle's legs just below the bottom of the wings. Apparently the basin-
ing process polished part of the center designs off these dies and
they had to be individually touched up. There is also evidence that
the A^2 reverse hub was reimpressed into some A^1 reverse dies caus-
ing some doubling of the design. The A^2 reverse apparently basin-
ed better than the A^1 reverse and required less individual touching
up of the dies.

Linderman was quite concerned over the slow progress in producing the working dies, since the Philadelphia mint urgently needed
them for producing in April the minimum 2,000,000 silver dollars
prescribed by the Bland-Allison Act. In today's terms, 2 million coins
a month seems a rather small figure but the Philadelphia Mint had,
until then, never struck coins at that rate.

In answer to a request by Linderman to Pollock on March 23 that
"Barber and Morgan report in writing their progress in making new
hubs and dies," Barber replied to Pollock (on the same day):

> The new hub commenced when the Director was here
> will be finished on the 28th of the Month and the dies
> therefrom I expect to ship on the 11th of April.

The second hub referred to in this letter was undoubtedly the new
obverse hub (fig. 6).

6. II Obv.   7. B Rev.

The new second design reverse hub had the eagle's tail feathers changed from eight to seven. Other changes in the reverse design included a smaller wreath and smaller olive branch leaves and was of lower relief (fig. 7).

"Efforts of Ingenuity" (7/8 TF)

Morgan further replied to Pollock on Monday, March 25:
> I beg to say that the new hub for reverse of silver dollar was finished and hardened today (March 25th). New dies from this hub will be ready about 2nd of April but I can enter this hub into the dies - fifty in number made from the old hub and have these ready this week.

This letter from Morgan clearly explains how the seven over eight tail feathers reverse dual hub originated. It was to be done as a matter of expediency, in order to save more than a week in obtaining the much needed working dies. That this short cut operation was indeed carried out is indicated by Morgan's letter to Linderman on March 26:
> Today I have made and finished dies from the new hub for reverse of silver dollar with reference to which I reported to you yesterday. These dies are now being used in the coining room by Mr. Downing - who is most competent to judge of these things - prefers to use them for a few days before he gives an opinion as to how the dies will work.

The purpose of the detailed background which has just been given is to provide conclusive evidence how and why the 7 over 8 tail feather variety occurred (fig. 8). (The seven over eight tail feather reverse shown is not unique as each modified die was different and it was not a basic design type.)

In summary, first, the new seven tail feather, parallel arrow feather (7 TF PAF) reverse hub of lower relief was entered into the old eight feather reverse die. Presumably, since the two reverses had border lettering that differed in position with respect to the eagle, the old die lettering, including the wreath, was ground and lapped away round the edge. When the new hub was entered into the old dies, only the center part of the design had a doubled appearance. Dies actually begin as cones in order to prevent the metal from spreading, cracking and chipping during each blow from the hub. Thus in order to finish the die in one or two blows from the hub, only the outer edge of the die could be ground away. Since about 50 reverse dies were modified, it is likely that on some of these dies the old design

8.

was probably completely removed and the eight tail feathers did not show beneath the seven tail feathers. Only 13 different dual hub B/A reverse die varieties are known. The other 37 A reverse dies may have been ground down sufficiently so that little of the original design remained. In addition, some of these B/A reverse dies may have been condemned at the Philadelphia mint and never used.

There is evidence that the lower relief, second design obverse hub was impressed on the old, higher relief obverse dies. These dual hub obverses have doubled stars, LIBERTY, symbol letters, and other design details.

Linderman, however, was still not satisfied with the coins. On April 5, he wrote a letter concerning the relief of the obverse silver dollar dies. Morgan replied on April 8:

> I have come to the conclusion that the head is well protected by the border when the dies do not sink or even when they sink a little, but when the dies sink as many of them did during the last month the heads come much too close together, and in some coins which have been issued they would actually touch.

Morgan went on to say:

> Although Mr. Barber does not appear to take any great interest in the finish of the dies himself, he has expressly forbidden Mr. Straub to receive any instructions from me.

From this letter it is apparent that Barber and Morgan were not on the best of terms, probably because of Linderman's special interest in the young Englishman and adoption of Morgan's design for the silver dollar. The dies that Morgan believed should not have been allowed in the presses were probably some of the seven over eight tail feather reverses and the double LIBERTY obverses. The letter also reveals that at the time the new seven tail feather dies were first used.

Linderman was still not completely satisfied with the design, as indicated by his letter to Pollock on April 10:

> I note a decided improvement in the execution of the silver dollar but I think there is room for some further slight improvement...

Linderman wrote to Pollack on April 15, ordering that the improvement be made:

> You expressed the opinion that further improvement in the new silver dollar is both practicable and desirable and the same can be accomplished without interfering with the several designs or impairing improvements already made.

The two different coin designs caused some concern to the public. There were various inquiries to the Treasury Department and the Philadelphia Mint pointing out the design differences and that they did not stack up to the same height. The main concern was whether the new design coin was genuine.

On May 17, Morgan reported to Linderman the progress on making the new dies:

> We have made two pairs of dies from the new hubs for

9. III Obv.   10. C Rev.

the silver dollar and tried them in the coining presses.
I understand that you have received a piece struck from
these dies.

The two new pairs of dies mentioned in this letter struck the first
coins of the third obverse and reverse designs (figs. 9-10). The C
reverse is the so-called 1878 P 7 TF SAF (slanted arrow feather) type.

The earliest date that the third design obverse and reverse dies
could have been used extensively is June 28, 1878. This design was
used for practically all later years of the Morgan dollar series. Because
of the large number of dies in the stockpile at that time, many different die marriages occurred.

Thus ended the remarkable story of the 1878 Morgan silver
dollars. For those who would choose to collect all of the 1878-P
varieties, it should be pointed out that as of this writing, there are
117 such varieties to whet one's collecting appetite.

[1]   The material contained in this paper has been abstracted from Leroy C. Van Allen
and A. George Mallis, *Comprehensive Catalogue and Encyclopedia of Morgan &
Peace Dollars*, Third Edition (Virginia Beach, 1992), Chapter 5.

[2]   "The Employment of George Morgan, Mint Engraver," *The Numismatic
Scrapbook Magazine* 1964, p. 310.

[3]   Letter from Morgan to Dr. Linderman, July 27, 1876, published in *NSM* (above,
n. 2), pp. 312-13.

[4]   Letter from Morgan to Dr. Linderman, September 18, 1876, Record Group 104,
National Archives.

[5]   Includes contributions on half and ten dollar pattern development by Pete R.
Bishal, for which the author is grateful.

[6]   Robert W. Julian, "History of Morgan Dollars," *Coin World*, September 26, 1984.

[7]   J.H. Judd, *United States Pattern, Experimental and Trial Pieces*, 6th ed. (Iola,
WI, 1977).

[8]   William S. Nawrocki, "Rare Galvanos," *COINage*, April 1984, pp. 32ff.

[9]   Reprinted by permission from Judd (above, n. 7).

[10]   Colonel Archibald Loudon Snowden had been Chief Coiner of the Philadelphia
Mint from 1866 to 1876. He was the son of the Director of the Mint from 1853 to
1861, James Ross Snowden.

The Silver Dollar as an Element
of International Trade:
A Study in Failure

John M. Kleeberg

Coinage of the Americas Conference
at the American Numismatic Society, New York

October 30, 1993

When the United States began the minting of silver dollars in 1794, it might reasonably have expected that the new coin would succeed in international trade.[1] The guldiner issued by Archduke Sigismund of the Tirol in 1486 is traditionally considered the first thaler. This was the first of many large silver crowns which circulated widely in international trade. It was followed by the issues of the Counts of Šlik at Joachimsthal around 1520, and finally by the introduction of a Spanish multiple of 8 reales sometime during the sixteenth century. Use of Spanish silver spread rapidly in China after the founding of Manila in 1572. By the seventeenth century, 8 reales from Spain and her American colonies were the chief coins in use in the China trade.[2] Useful confirmation of this is provided by four Chinese hoards of Spanish and Spanish colonial coins, which were probably imported into China between 1645 and 1690.[3] The China trade was an unbalanced trade, a silver drain; Europe wanted tea, porcelain, spices, and silks, and the Chinese, who in many ways were more advanced than the Europeans, wanted nothing from Europe—the only thing they required was silver. Nor were all silver coins acceptable to the Chinese. Although many European trading companies tried to introduce imitation 8 reales of their own into the China trade—such as the portcullis crown of the British East India Company, or the Emden trade thaler of the Königlich Preussische Asiatische Compagnie von Emden, there is no evidence that any of the coins were widely accepted in China, and (in the case of the portcullis crown) good evidence that they were rejected.[4]

If we were to map (figs. 1 and 2) the finds of Spanish-American silver coins, there would be few parts of the world where they would not penetrate. The only major exception would be the Baltic and its eastern European hinterland. This was because some trades developed their own specialized coins. The Levant trade used the Dutch leeuwendaalder; the Baltic trade first the rijksdaalder, later the patagon, and these coins were themselves subject to imitation.[5] The Dutch, who have always been one of the most sophisticated trading nations, minted special silver crowns for special trades: the ducaton for the East India trade, the rijksdaalder for the Baltic, the leeuwendaalder for the Levant, and the patagon (or kruisdaalder, or Albertusthaler) for domestic transactions.[6] The Banks of Hamburg and Amsterdam tariffed the less fine patagon (or kruisdaalder, or Albertusthaler) at the same rate as the old rijksdaalder, so by 1700 it drove out the rijksdaalder in the Baltic trade. The trade in the Baltic and much of Eastern Europe was dominated by this large silver coin, to the exclusion of the Spanish-American 8 real.[7] There was

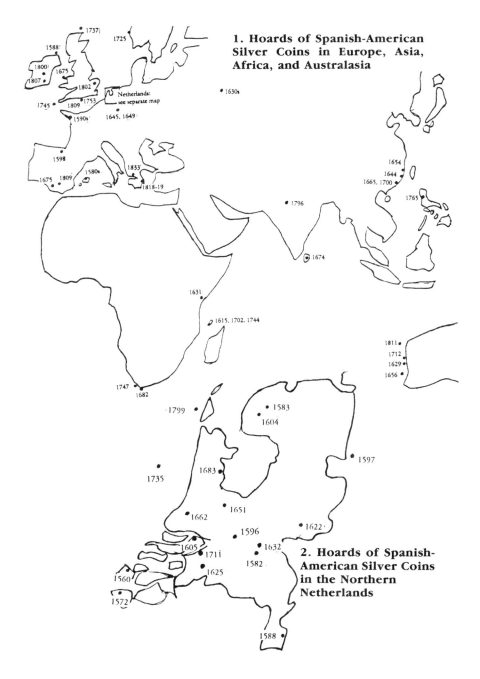

1. Hoards of Spanish-American Silver Coins in Europe, Asia, Africa, and Australasia

2. Hoards of Spanish-American Silver Coins in the Northern Netherlands

good precedent for the striking of coins in imitation of successful trade dollars, although not all of these attempts proved to be successful.

Everything seemed to favor a wide acceptance for the United States silver dollar. Its likeness was not too different from the Carolus dollars, or 8 real pieces with the image of King Charles III of Spain, which were then the most widely accepted coin in southern China. By 1796 the U.S. silver dollar had reached China, and was described in the minutes of the British East India Company:

> The dollars brought by the Americans are a National Coin agreeing precisely in weight with the Spanish Dollar, but on assay have a few Cash more of alloy; they are stamped with the Head of General Washington with fifteen stars and the motto of "Liberty" dated 1795, and have on the Reverse an Eagle surrounded with Laurels and the Motto "United States of America."[8]

The evidence we have for the circulation of the United States silver dollar outside the United States is of three kinds. First of all, literary evidence; secondly, countermarks; and thirdly, hoards.

Our literary evidence for the circulation of the United States silver dollar is provided by money changer manuals, or cambists, which describe or depict the United States silver dollar. One of the most widely quoted cambists is the beautiful work by Pierre-Frédéric Bonneville, published at Paris at 1806. Many later cambists cribbed their information from Bonneville. It looks as though Bonneville actually saw most of the coins he chose to depict, and he seems to have been careful to show all the major types: flowing hair and draped bust, large eagle, small eagle, and heraldic eagle (figs. 3, 4, and 5). There is, however, one major fault: Eric Newman has pointed out that Bonneville depicts a 1798 half dollar, a non-existent coin. Bon-

3.

4.

5.

neville also took over the edge lettering of the dollar wholesale and applied it to the half dollar. If Bonneville is accurate in depicting the silver dollars, he errs in his account of the gold coins, and appears to be the source of the error in early cambists which call the eagle a double eagle, and the half eagle an eagle.[9] Bonneville is the earliest work to depict a United States silver dollar that I have come across, although Eric Newman has discovered an earlier (1796) depiction of a United States coin (a 1795 eagle with thirteen leaves below the eagle; the variety may be a Breen.2-A).[10]

Rather different in quality is the work by the goldsmith James Ede, published in London in 1808. Ede depicts a bust dollar, to which he assigns the date 1793 (fig. 6). Further comment is, I think, superfluous.[11]

Patrick Kelly, writing in 1821, gave a valid description of a dollar of 1795, but appears never to have seen a heraldic eagle dollar. He writes, "On the reverse of pieces of 1795 &c. the Eagle is entirely surrounded with branches of palm and laurel." He also says that

6.

"the inferior coins [i.e., below a dollar] have no letters on the edge," which indicates that he certainly never saw a half dollar, to say nothing of letter edged cents and half cents.[12]

Christian Noback's cambist, published at Rudolstadt in Thuringia in 1833,[13] is important as a means of transmission from Bonneville to the 1858 cambist of Frey and Blaser (fig. 7). The cambist of Xaver Frey and C. Blaser, published at Berne in Switzerland in 1858, has a woodcut that makes Liberty look very unpleasant (fig. 8). A com-

7.

8.

parison of their depiction of the 1795 dollar with those in Christian Noback and Bonneville makes it clear that Noback copied his depiction of the 1795 dollar from Bonneville, and Frey and Blaser copied their depiction from Noback. The position of the edge lettering is the same in all three pictures; certain errors in the depiction of the edge decoration are carried over from picture to picture; and the unpleasant facial expression begins in Noback and is exaggerated in Frey and Blaser. So of these three cambists, only Bonneville saw an actual coin. Frey and Blaser base much of their information on Congressional legislation, so they thought that the United States struck dollars from 1786 to 1792. They also assume that dollars of the draped bust type were struck from 1792 until 1837.[14]

In 1858 Christian Noback, this time assisted by his son Friedrich, issued another mercantile reference work: the *Münz-, Maas- und Gewichtsbuch.* On page 519, the Nobacks say that the silver dollar was no longer being struck. This was 18 years after the striking of silver dollars had resumed, and clearly the Nobacks had yet to see one. The Nobacks also list as circulating coins some coins we consider patterns: the ring dollars and the ring cents. Although the Nobacks seem very accurate when discussing monetary matters in Rudolstadt or Königsberg, their account of silver dollars is incorrect. On the other hand, they provide a very good listing of California gold.[15]

Matters did not improve with time. The publishing house of von Vangerow in Bremerhaven issued a second edition of their cambist in 1868. This cambist illustrates a flowing hair dollar of 1795—with a small eagle reverse (fig. 9).[16]

The cambists, in short, are full of peculiar errors. Eric Newman has drawn attention to a cambist of Urosius Andreits, published in Budapest in 1832, which even goes so far as to depict an 1804 dollar—two years before the U.S. Mint created that fantasy piece.[17] United States coins were made in only small amounts, and were rare-

9.

10.

THE GHOST of a DOLLAR or the BANKERS SURPRIZE

ly seen; so it is not surprising that many errors crept into descriptions of the coins. Some authors, like Ede, went so far as to depict coins they had not seen. Others, like Kelly, made broad assertions which were untrue. Many cambists copied uncritically from each other, making engravings or woodcuts not from actual coins, but from engravings and woodcuts in other cambists. The errors in the cambists are evidence for the small circulation of United States coins outside the borders of the United States.

A useful literary confirmation of the overwhelming proportion of Spanish dollars, presumably from Mexico, is provided by a caricature of one of the most important bankers of the early Republic, Stephen Girard, who is fantasizing about seeing a dollar (fig. 10). When Girard fantasizes about a dollar, he thinks about a Mexican 8 real with the head of Charles IV—not a United States dollar. The caricaturist could reasonably suppose, in other words, that the most important banker of the early Republic, and a banker who operated out of the very city in which the mint was located, when imagining a dollar would think of a Mexican dollar.[18]

The second form of evidence we have for circulation of the silver dollar outside the United States is countermarks on silver dollars. Professor Robert Stark has enumerated the countermarks on silver dollars, foreign as well as domestic.[19] There are, to my knowledge, only thirteen early United States silver dollars in existence with foreign countermarks (including doubtful pieces), and two early United States dollars which were overstruck. One of the counter-marked pieces is a dollar of 1794 with a Philippine countermark of 1811, which has not been seen since it disappeared during the Japanese occupation of the Philippines in 1941.[20] A United States dollar of 1795 has the Bank of England countermark of 1797-1803. Two of 1798 and two (or three) of 1799 have the octagonal counter-mark of 1804. Although Michael Dolley contended that a 1798 dollar in the British Museum appeared genuine when the bust on the countermark was compared with the bust on the silver penny, Frederick Pridmore was suspicious of the authenticity of all of these pieces. In the case of one of the 1799 dollars Pridmore said outright that the countermark was not consistent with the silver penny.[21] Frederick M. Rose's useful pamphlet on chopmarks depicts a chop-marked 1799 dollar (Bolender 21).[22] There is an 1800 dollar (Bolender.11) in the ANS collection with fleur-de-lis countermarks from Puerto Rico, used by the collectors of customs at the major Puerto Rican ports, to guarantee dollars which had been holed (ANS coin number 1913.130.35, gift of Howland Wood, November 13, 1913).[23] There are also three private British countermarks of the period of the Napoleonic wars on United States silver dollars.[24] One of these, an 1800 dollar (Bolender.10a) countermarked by J. & J. W. of Hurlet in Renfrewshire, has been attributed to John Wilson and is in the ANS collection, (1967.57.1, part gift of the Norweb Collection and purchase from B. Seaby & Son, November 30, 1966).[25] Harrington Manville is doubtful of the authenticity of this piece; he has written:

> The J. & J. W. Hurlet mark of the Copperas Coal Co. in Hurlet, Renfrewshire was discovered only in 1951 but in the next twenty years at least ten specimens have appeared—from two different dies and including one on an American dollar. Although one or both types may have been produced in early in the nineteenth century, their sudden appearance in several varieties is, at the least, suspicious.[26]

Brunk, on the other hand, has said that "the countermark that includes a triangle of three dots is almost certainly original."[27] The United States dollar does have this triangle of three dots.

The question of the authenticity of this countermark, as of so many others, is a problematic one; but it has no effect upon my conclusions. The total number of silver coins countermarked by private issuers in Britain during the Napoleonic era, surviving to the present day, is about 800. Of these, there are three countermarks on United States silver dollars. Whether all three are genuine, or all three are fake, makes no matter; the point is that the number of surviving United States silver dollars countermarked in England, Scotland, and Ireland, is less than one half of one percent of surviving countermarked coins, with most of the other countermarks occurring on Spanish colonial silver. This suggests that the number of United States silver dollars which were in circulation in Britain and Ireland in this period was also minuscule.

An equally problematic area of countermarking is the West Indies. The only United States dollar with a West Indies countermark (the Puerto Rican examples excluded) is a cut out Guadeloupe holey dollar, about which there can be little doubt that it is a modern fake.[28] In the West Indies, the United States silver dollar and the Mexican silver dollar traded at par, even though the United States silver dollar had slightly less silver. It was supposed to be profitable for merchants to engage in an "endless chain": ship United States silver dollars to the West Indies and exchange them for Mexican dollars. This export of United States silver dollars was the reason the Mint ceased to produce them after 1803, and why Jefferson formally suspended their minting in 1806.[29] Why are there not more United States silver dollars which were cut and countermarked in the West Indies, if the United States coins were gradually driving out the Mexican ones?

One explanation may be that the authorities in the West Indies wanted to keep the Mexican silver in the country, and the United States coins out; they cut and countermarked the Mexican pieces, and rejected the United States coins. Another explanation may be that the endless chain or no, the United States silver dollar was still a very scarce coin, and the tiny amounts made by the first United States Mint were totally swamped by the huge production of Mexico.

A rather unusual use of the United States silver dollar occurred in Montevideo, Uruguay. There the country was besieged by the Argentine troops of General Rosas for nine years, which Alexandre Dumas père called "the modern siege of Troy." During this siege, emergency issues of pesos were made by the Montevideans. Women handed over their jewelry, men the saddle decorations of their horses, priests the crosses of the churches, and all were melted down to make the coins. At least five coins are known overstruck on other coins. At least two such pesos are overstruck on early United States dollars.[30] One of them, a 1798 dollar (it appears to be a Bolender.8; the Uruguay reference is Silvera.7.1.1) is in the ANS collection, (1987.81.42, the gift of Howard W. Herz).[31] The undertype of the siege peso in the ANS collection has a visible date—1798. Although this is another example of an exported United States silver dollar, these silver dollars are only two examples, compared with other, more common undertypes. Furthermore, the ANS example has prooflike surfaces, which suggests that it saw no circulation at all, but was a prestige issue made for local dignitaries. It is interesting to note that the number of such coins known—five—corresponds almost exactly to the number given out at the ceremony when the Montevideo mint was opened, namely four. One peso apiece was given to the President of the Republic, the Interior Minister, the Minister of War and the Finance Minister. The other coin known would have gone to someone like Don Andrés Lamas, the governor of Montevideo, who helped set up the mint. The mint had much trouble purifying the silver brought in, and was trying to use cupolation.[32] This provides a simple explanation why the mint overstruck these coins. It needed to make presentation pieces in time for the ceremony, and the best possible planchets were existing coins—including two United States silver dollars.

The third form of evidence we have available to us is hoards. An argument *e silentio* is a weak one, but the United States silver dollar is absent from nearly all foreign hoards of this period known to me. The Wellington Bridge (1954) hoard, for example, which was found in Ireland, had a closing date of 1807. It contained 143 silver coins; 70 of these were 8 reales from Mexico, Lima, and Potosí. There was not a single United States coin in the hoard.[33]   To my knowledge, there is one, and only one, foreign find of coins of this period which contains United States silver dollars. This is a shipwreck found at Point Cloates off the coast of Western Australia, known as the *Rapid*, which sank in 1811. The *Rapid* is extremely interesting for us, because it is a United States merchant ship, which had left the port of Boston. It gives a good idea of the silver trade coins available for a ship about to leave Boston for China. 20,000 silver dollar size coins were found in the *Rapid*. Of these coins, 13 were United States silver dollars. The proportion of 20,000 eight reales to 13 U.S. dollars is rather overwhelming. And this is on a ship which set out from Boston![34]

Another hoard which is suggestive in indicating the scarcity of the United States silver dollar is the Donner Lake, California (1891) hoard. An 8 reales of Mexico, dated 1845, closes the hoard. Every

11. The Donner Lake, CA (1891) Hoard

Buried by Mary Graves, December 1846

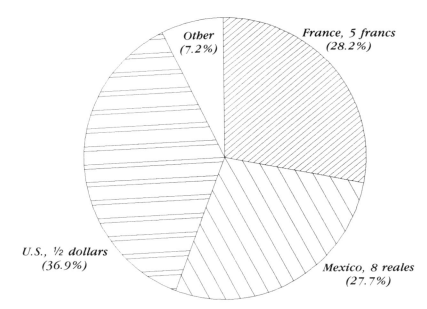

Other *(7.2%)*

France, 5 francs *(28.2%)*

U.S., ½ dollars *(36.9%)*

Mexico, 8 reales *(27.7%)*

indication justifies the assumption that this hoard was buried by Mrs. Mary Graves, a member of the Donner party, on or before December 16, 1846, when the party abandoned the camp at the lake. The story of the Donner party, the pioneers who were caught in the snows of the Sierra Nevada and resorted to cannibalism, is well known. What is of interest is the composition of the hoard (fig. 11). A remarkable aspect is the predominance of French five franc pieces, which is unexpected. The large number of United States half dollars is what we would expect, for the half dollar was the true workhorse coin of the early United States. The early United States mint devoted its effort to one denomination in each metal: for copper, it was the cent; for silver, the half dollar; and for gold, the half eagle. Most significant is the total absence of the United States silver dollar from this hoard—even though minting of the coin had resumed in 1840—and its replacement in monetary circulation not only by Mexican 8 reales and U.S. half dollars, which we expect, but also by French five franc pieces.[35]

The literary evidence, the countermarks and overstrikes, and the hoard evidence all combine to suggest that the United States silver dollar before 1860 had only a tiny circulation within the United States itself, and an infinitesimal circulation outside of the United States.

In the 1860s a number of factors prevented Mexico from supplying dollars to the China trade. First of all, the adventure of Maximilian in Mexico resulted in great turmoil, which cut the production of the Mexican mints. Secondly, both Maximilian and his opponents changed the design of the eight reales piece, renaming it the peso. The Chinese, always sensitive to the slightest change in design, rejected the new coins. Furthermore, after the Republican defeat of Maximilian, an export tax of about 12% was levied on each peso exported.[36] These changes made it attractive for other countries to begin minting their own silver coins for the China trade. The first of these was Britain, which began minting trade dollars for Hong Kong. These were not particularly successful, partly because Chinese merchants liked to chop the coins, and some of them feared that placing a chop on Queen Victoria might be considered *lèse majesté*. Many chopmarks are placed over the eyes of the head on the coins. This may be related to the way the Chinese perceived the portraits—as pictures of devils. The Chinese called the Carolus dollar "Gwei-mien," or "Devil's face," the U.S. trade dollar a "Devil's head."[37] A traditional method of counteracting an evil influence is to knock out its eyes—compare the western superstition of the evil eye. So the tendency to chopmark the eyes may very well be intentional.

The second nation to mint its own trade dollar was Japan, which began to mint a silver yen with the China trade in mind. The third nation was the United States.

John Willem has covered the history of the U.S. trade dollar extremely well in his superb book.[38] The United States trade dollar was not a failure—in China. In China it experienced a modest success. Some 25 million trade dollars were exported to China. Although the trade dollar made no headway in the north of China and in the interior, it was readily accepted in the southern ports and in the Philippines. Dr. de Jesus writes that trade dollars of the dates 1873-78 were common at one time in Manila but became scarcer as more were melted to make silverware and jewelry; the most common trade dollar in Manila coin and jewelry shops was, unsurprisingly, 1877-S.[39] Many trade dollars did see circulation, as we can tell from their chopmarks: in fact, chopmarked examples are known of all date and mintmark combinations of the years 1873-78, including the overmintmark combination 1875-S over CC.[40] They also occur in large numbers in Chinese hoards.[41]

The trade dollar, however, ended as an abject failure—not because of its career in China, but because of what happened in the United States. In the 1870s huge new silver deposits were discovered in Nevada. At the same time, Germany and the Scandinavian countries adopted the gold standard. Old silver thalers (many dating from the eighteenth century) were turned into the Reichsbank in exchange for the new gold marks. The German government estimated that it had 5,500 metric tons of pure silver superfluous to its needs. Not all of this was sold at once—in 1879 the German government stopped the sales—but from 1873 until then Germany sold off 3,551.5 metric tons of pure silver, the equivalent of 147,567,208 standard silver dollars. Until 1876 this difficult task was entrusted to the newly founded Deutsche Bank, which had been established to specialize in foreign trade and in the person of Hermann Wallich had someone with direct experience of Asian markets. Wallich had served as the Shanghai branch manager of a French bank, the Comptoir d'Escompte. The Deutsche Bank disposed of 1,100 metric tons of silver. Most of it was sold into the London and Hamburg silver markets, but over 250 metric tons were sold directly in the East, in Bombay, Calcutta and Shanghai. The lovely old thalers were melted into bars before they were sold into the silver market. The one liquidation conducted in the form of coins was French 5 franc pieces which had formed part of the French indemnity or were found in the government tills when the German administration took over Alsace-Lorraine. Wallich presented these 5 franc pieces directly in Paris. After 1876 the Reichsbank took over the sales from the Deutsche Bank, selling most of the silver in London to English banks. The Deutsche Bank had done quite well out of the business, and the Reichsbank wanted the profits for itself. Alas, the Reichsbank was disappointed; either because of its lack of skill or because the silver price gave way quite dramatically in 1877 and 1878, the Reichsbank suffered heavy losses and had to stop the sales in 1879.[42]

These various events combined to depress the silver price. The trade dollar, which in 1873 contained slightly more than a dollar's worth of silver, by 1876 was worth little more than eighty cents. The United States accordingly revoked the legal tender status of the trade dollar.[43]

At this point a crucial error by the United States government became very important. Colonies tend to be cash poor compared with the metropolis. Colonial coins often have a higher valuation than metropolitan issues. It is a traditional law of colonial monetary policy that colonial coins must have a distinguishing mark so that they do not get into circulation in the mother country. Portugal, for example, prevented the circulation of Brazilian coins by giving them peculiar denominations such as 320, 480, or 960. For years Britain enforced the rule that the monarch must always wear a crown on colonial issues, and be bareheaded on metropolitan ones. The United States, when creating a coin for export, ignored this rule, and created a coin which looked very much like a domestic United States silver dollar. It was possible for unscrupulous employers to buy the dollars at eighty cents, and put them in the pay packets of their workers with the valuation of a dollar. In 1887 the United States finally made good on its obligations, and redeemed the trade dollars by exchanging them for standard silver dollars—Morgan dollars—which were legal tender. Over 7.5 million trade dollars were redeemed this way.[44]

Although the United States trade dollar was a failure, it was a failure for domestic reasons. Its potential for the China trade remained, and other countries imitated it. In 1874 the Japanese began to issue their own trade dollar, of the same weight and fineness as the United States one. In the 1890s, when the Mexicans finally adopted the name peso for their coin and began to export fewer pesos at the same time, other countries began minting trade dollars to fill the gap. The French began by minting a piastre de commerce for their territories in French Indochina. In 1921 this coin was struck for the French account at the San Francisco Mint, thereby giving a second life to a trade dollar from a United States mint. The British, too, resumed minting of a trade dollar, this time at Calcutta. The output of the British trade dollar was huge—over 21.5 million in 1898, over 30.5 million in 1899. In 1900 the amount minted dropped to over 9 million for obvious reasons, namely the outbreak of the Boxer rebellion.[45] Rather oddly, however, the Boxer rebellion expanded the area of acceptance of the British trade dollar. Dr. Knappe, the Imperial German Consul at Shanghai, wrote on October 3, 1900:

> In consequence of the massing of troops the demand for silver dollars has become very great and hence they have increased 10% in price. The English banks have used this opportunity to introduce the English dollar, which until now has always been refused here. The Hong Kong & Shanghai Banking Corporation is said to have brought 4 million such dollars to China, and the Deutsch-Asiatische Bank has also paid some of the sums requested from it by the troops in English dollars.[46]

In 1901 over 27 million British trade dollars were minted; in 1902, over 31 million British trade dollars were minted.[47]

The Morgan dollar, which began mintage the same year the trade dollar ceased to be minted for circulation, was not usually sought after as an international trade coin. The one time when it was exported on a large scale was during the inflationary period of the First World War, when all silver disappeared from circulation. The largest single export of silver dollars—265 million silver dollars— was the intergovernment transaction between Britain and the United States during the First World War when Britain needed silver bullion for India. These Morgan dollars were not, however, exported as dollars. They were melted first into silver bricks of 1,000 ounces apiece, and then sent in trains with armed guards across the continent to San Francisco, where they were loaded onto ships.[48] The private sector in China was another big purchaser of silver from the United States in 1919-20, and some of the silver was exported in the form of dollars, rather than as bullion bars.[49] Generally speaking, however, the Morgan dollars only languished in Treasury vaults. Some Morgan dollars did make their way to Puerto Rico, where they received the fleur-de-lis counterstamp. Occasional Morgan and Peace dollars do turn up with chopmarks, but these are oddities.[50]

In 1896 the experiment of the United States with silver coinage was the major issue of the presidential election. McKinley and the gold standard won the election. The gold standard became law in the United States in 1900. Yet history is filled with peculiar ironies: for McKinley was to be responsible for the introduction of another United States minted, circulating silver dollar on the territory of the United States.

As a result of the Spanish-American War of 1898, the United States acquired a colonial empire, including the Philippines. The United States thereby occupied a country with a very complicated currency system; the *Manila Times* called Philippine currency:

> an extremely mixed-up affair, so mixed up that it constituted the study of a lifetime, and various people who devoted their lives to the study of it used to make money of it at the expense of people whose time was otherwise occupied...at all times and under all circumstances the banks, exchange brokers and a few clever Chinese and others managed to juggle with the fluctuations in change and currency legislation so as to score always.[51]

This description is colored by Sinophobia, but it does express the suspicion and hostility which many Filipinos felt, and which came to be shared by the U.S. troops. The continuing warfare against Aguinaldo tied down a large United States army of occupation. The troops were paid in gold dollars, or in paper money backed with gold dollars. This, however, was no good in the Philippines, where only silver was used, and the local banks, including the Hong Kong & Shanghai Banking Corporation and the Chartered Bank of India, Australia and China, would convert these gold dollars into silver dollars before they would accept deposits. The soldiers complained greatly about the foreign exchange fees.

The Filipinos similarly were confused by the introduction of the U.S. Morgan dollar, which, because it was tied to gold, was worth two pesos at the official rate even though it contained less silver than a peso. The United States government authorities considered several solutions. One proposal was to pay the troops in Mexican silver dollars. This was rejected because a lieutenant's weekly pay would then weigh 29 pounds, and a colonel's 73 pounds.

The idea of introducing U.S. coins was considered and rejected. The United States, in the person of Charles A. Conant, finally adopted the suggestions of the British overseas banks, and introduced the system which had worked well in India, namely the gold exchange standard. John Maynard Keynes has written that "In dealing with her dependencies, she [the United States] has herself imitated, almost slavishly, India."[52] In other words, for foreign exchange purposes the country was on a gold standard, but domestically only silver would be used. There was no free coinage of silver. In 1903 this was put into force with the introduction of the Philippine peso (the "conant peso"), which was fixed to the United States dollar at a value of two pesos to one United States gold dollar.[53]

The gold exchange standard proved to be a very influential idea. Having put it into practice in the Philippines, the United States also used it when it reorganized the currencies of Panama and Mexico ("dollar diplomacy"). Keynes spoke quite highly of the gold exchange standard in his first published book, *Indian Currency and Finance* (1913). It was widely used in the interwar period as a substitute for the pure gold standard, and many of its concepts were taken up when Keynes and others established the Bretton Woods system in 1944.

Unfortunately, the United States government got it wrong again. A gold exchange standard could work in India with little problem, because India was relatively self-sufficient. The Philippines, however, lie opposite southern China, and in its economic sphere of influence. If the trade dollar had been overvalued versus its bullion value, so that trade dollars flooded into the United States, the new Philippines peso was drastically undervalued in terms of bullion, so the peso fled the Philippines, many going across the Manila straits to China, as numerous chopmarked examples attest.

The government accordingly reduced the size of the Philippine peso in 1907, so that it would be worth more than its bullion weight, and this adjustment seems to have worked.

The history of the United States silver dollar, as an international trade coin, was a history of failure. Why?

First of all, for the greater part of its early history the United States did not produce much silver. It could not make many silver coins: the United States only minted $1,758,493 worth of all five silver denominations (half dimes, dimes, quarter dollars, half dollars, and dollars) between 1794 and 1803. By contrast, the Mexican mint turned out $211,991,719 worth of silver coin in that same period.[54]

The amount of silver coined by the Mexican mint each year was more than ten times the entire silver coinage of the United States mint in 1794-1803. Furthermore, so long as Mexican coins were just as good as United States silver dollars, there was no inducement for merchants to bring them to the mint to recoin them into United States silver dollars: they would have lost interest on their money. (The interest lost while waiting for Mexican dollars to be recoined into U.S. dollars is often insufficiently emphasized as a reason for small mintages in the early years of the Republic. Willem, for example, does not mention it.)

Thirdly, by the time the United States began to produce silver in large quantities, it had fallen out of favor as a currency standard, replaced by gold monometallism. Only in China was silver still widely accepted, and the United States acted ineptly, creating a coin which was easily introduced into circulation in the domestic market. The United States did produce one very popular trade coin for the nineteenth century: this was the gold double eagle, which remains a popular asset outside the United States, not least among Swiss banks. But it did not succeed in producing a silver trade coin.

Finally, after the United States had itself adopted the gold standard, it was compelled to reintroduce a circulating silver dollar size coin into one of its territories, namely the Philippines. But even in the Philippines, in silver's classic area of circulation, the United States government could not get the gold-silver ratio right, and had to reduce the size of the coin, until it was smaller than the classic silver dollar.

[1] The author would like to thank Kenneth Bressett, Emmett McDonald, Eric Newman, Jules Reiver, Marcos Silvera, and Robert Stark for their assistance and comments.

[2] John M. Willem, *The United States Trade Dollar: America's Only Unwanted, Unhonored Coin* (Racine, WI, 1965) pp. 26-27, 30-31.

[3] J.E. Cribb, "Some Hoards of Spanish Coins of the Seventeenth Century Found in Fukien Province, China," *Coin Hoards* 3 (1977), pp. 180-84.

[4] Willem (above, n. 2), pp. 26-27, 179-80; Wolfgang Hess and Dietrich Klose, eds.,*Vom Taler zum Dollar 1486-1986* (Munich, 1986), especially pp. 187-94, "Der spanische Piaster als Welthandelsmünze und die von ihm abgeleiteten Grossilbermünzen"; John Porteous, *Coins in History* (New York, 1969) p. 208.

[5] *Vom Taler zum Dollar* (above, n. 4), pp. 97-102, 129-31.

[6] H. Enno van Gelder, *De Nederlandse Munten* (Utrecht/Antwerp, 1965), pp. 108-10, 149-50; Glendining sale cat., Oct. 28, 1969 (The *De Liefde* Treasure, see esp. the preface by John Porteous); H. Enno van Gelder, "De Munten van 'De Liefde'," *Jaarboek voor Munt- en Penningkunde*, 56/57 (1969/70), pp. 63-74; Porteous, (above, n. 4), pp. 187-90, 209.

[7] *Vom Taler zum Dollar* (above, n. 4), pp. 129-31; for examples of the occurrence of these Dutch coins in finds in the Ukraine, see the inventory of Ukrainian modern coin hoards: Mikołaj Kotlar, *Znaleziska Monet z XIV-XVII w. na Obszarze Ukraińskiej SRR. Materiały* (Warsaw, 1975).

[8] Hosea Ballou Morse, *The Chronicles of the East India Company Trading to China 1635-1834* (Cambridge, MA, 1926), vol. 2, p. 280; Willem (above, n. 2), pp. 44-45.

[9] Pierre-Frédéric Bonneville, *Traité des Monnaies d'Or et d'Argent qui Circulent chez les Différens Peuples; Examinées Sous les Rapports du Poids, du Titre et de la Valeur Réelle, Avec leurs Diverses Empreintes* (Paris, 1806), pp. 229-30, and the two pls. following; Eric P. Newman, "Earliest Illustration of an Unknown 1804 U.S. Dollar," *The Numismatist* 1990, pp. 1596, 1657. Newman's article provides a good survey of many cambists and their non-existent U.S. coins. I have added here a few additional cambists, mostly German and Swiss.

[10] Chauncey Lee, *The American Accomptant; Being a Plain, Practical and Systematic Compendium of Federal Arithmetic; in Three Parts: Designed for the Use of Schools, and Specially Calculated for the Commercial Meridian of the United States of America* (Lansingburgh, NY, 1797). Beneath the various coins depicted, an early hand has written "10" below the eagle and "3.074" below the Brazilian 1/2 moidore (2000 reis) of 1715, Bahia mint. Many thanks to Eric Newman for sharing this information with me.

[11] James Ede, *A View of the Gold & Silver Coins of All Nations Exhibited In Above Four Hundred Copper Plate Engravings Correctly Executed by an Eminent Artist to Which is Added in a Regular Index, the Name, Assay, Weight and Value of Each; Also Sir Isaac Newton's Tables of Foreign Gold & Silver Coins, Made in the Year*

1700, by Order of the Privy Council (London, 1808), pl. 4. A handwritten note in the ANS copy says that it is the second edition. Newman (above, n. 9), pp. 1595, 1657-58.

[12]   P. Kelly, *The Universal Cambist and Commercial Instructor; Being a Full and Accurate Treatise on the Exchanges, Monies, Weights, and Measures, of All Trading Nations and Their Colonies; With an Account of their Banks, Public Funds, and Paper Currencies. The Second Edition, Including A Revision of Foreign Weights and Measures, From an Actual Comparison of Their Standards, by the Order and Aid of the British Government* (London, 1821), vol. 2, p. 213.

[13]   Christian Noback, *Vollständiges Handbuch der Münz-, Bank- und Wechsel-Verhältnisse aller Länder und Handelsplätze der Erde. Enthaltend: eine ausführliche, auf die neuesten bewährtesten Angaben und Untersuchungen gegründete, Darstellung der Rechnungsmünzen, der wirklich geprägten Gold-, Platina- und Silber-Münzen, so wie der bestehenden Bank-Anstalten und der Kurs-Systeme, oder der Wechsel-, Geld- und Staats-Papier-Kurse, Wechselusanzen und der haupt-sächlichsten Wechsel-Ordnungen, nebst Angabe der Messen und Messgebräuche der bedeutendsten Handels- und Wechselplätze. Mit getreuen Abbildungen der vornehmsten Gold-, Platina und Silbermünzen aller Länder. [In 380 Münzbildern auf 119 Tafeln.] Für alle diejenigen, denen eine umfassende Kenntniss des Münz-, Bank- und Wechselwesens unentbehrlich ist* (Rudolstadt, 1833), vol. 3, pls. 81, 82.

[14]   Xaver Frey and C. Blaser, *Münzbuch, oder Abbildung der kursirenden Geldsorten; mit genauer Angabe: ihres Gehalts in französischer alter und neuer, und in deutscher Bezeichnungsweise; ihres Gewichts in französischen Grän und Grammen, und ihres Werths in französischer und in alter Schweizerwährung, im deutschen 20 und 24½ Gulden- und 14 Thalerfuss. Nebst einer Übersicht der wichtigsten Rechnungsmünzen. Mit deutschem und französischem Text. Zweite, ganz umgeänderte und stark vermehrte Ausgabe. Nach den zuverlässigsten ältern und neuern Quellen bearbeitet* (Berne, 1856), pp. 245-46, 658.

[15]   Christian Noback and Friedrich Noback, *Münz-, Maass- und Gewichtsbuch. Das Geld-, Maass- und Wechselwesen, die Kurse, Staatspapiere, Banken, Handelsanstalten und Usanzen aller Staaten und wichtigern Orte* (Leipzig, 1858) p. 519. Strictly speaking, this is not a cambist. It is also not a second edition of the 1833 Noback cambist published at Rudolstadt. When a new edition of the *Münz-, Maass- und Gewichtsbuch* appeared in 1879, the new edition was called the second edition, not the third.

[16]   *Das Münzen-Buch oder die im Weltverkehr coursirenden, gängigsten Gold- und Silber-Münzen aller Welttheile und Staaten in natürlicher Grösse und Zeichnung. Ein in alphabetischer Reihenfolge, so wie unter Berücksichtigung der neuesten Geographie geordnetes Hülfsmittel für den Unterricht und zur Selbstbelehrung. Zugleich ein praktisches Werth-Nachschlagebuch für Geschäfts- und Handels- Kreise über die gegenwärtig im Verkehr befindlichen Gold- und Silber-Münzen aller Länder nach ihrem Werth in Preuss. Courant, in Oesterreichischer und Süddeutscher Gulden-Währung* (Bremerhaven, 1868), p. 112. The introduction says that this is the se-cond edition of a book first published in 1858.

[17]   Newman (above, n. 9), pp. 1592-96, 1659-60.

[18]   Bernard F. Reilly, Jr., *American Political Prints, 1766-1876. A Catalog of the*

Collections in the Library of Congress (Boston, 1991), pp. 11-12, no. 1808-2. The title of the caricature is "The Ghost of a Dollar or the Bankers Surprize."

[19] Robert Stark, "Countermarks on Early U.S. Dollars," *John Reich Journal* 8 (1993), pp. 27-39. Two foreign countermarks not included in this article are the Philippines countermark on the 1794 dollar and the chopmarked 1800 dollar which Rose lists. The article also does not mention the two Montevidean siege pesos which have early dollars as their undertype.

[20] Dr. P. I. de Jesus, "U.S. Coins in the Philippines," *The Numismatist* 1952, pp. 354-57.

[21] Howland Wood, "The Bank of England Counterstamp on United States Money," *The Numismatist* 1904, pp. 357-59; R.H.M. Dolley, "A 1798 United States Dollar with the George III Octagonal Countermark," *The Numismatic Circular* 63 (1955), p. 59; F. Pridmore, "The Bank of England Oval and Octagonal Countermarked Token Dollars of 1797-1804. Forgeries and Concoctions," *The Numismatic Circular* 63 (1955), pp. 307-11; Stark (above, n. 19), pp. 28-29. It is not clear whether the 1799 with the octagonal countermark mentioned by Wood is identical with one of those mentioned by Dolley. There can thus be at least two or three 1799 dollars with octagonal countermarks.

[22] F.M. Rose, *Chopmarks* (Dallas, 1987), p. 24, fig. 85. I owe this reference to Emmett McDonald.

[23] Jaime Gonzalez, *A Puerto Rican Counterstamp*, ANSNNM 88 (New York, 1940), which also depicts coin 1913.130.35; Stark (above, n. 19), p. 28, is another depiction of 1913.130.35; Maurice M. Gould and Lincoln W. Higgie, *1962 Catalog of the Money of Puerto Rico* (Racine, WI, 1962), pp. 10-13, esp. p. 13 depicting two more countermarked silver dollars, one a Morgan dollar of 1880, the other a trade dollar of 1876. The mints are not visible. In *A Puerto Rican Counterstamp*, Jaime Gonzalez mentioned that he had countermarked coins of those same denominations and dates in his collection. He also says that Robert R. Prann had two coins of those same denominations and dates in his collection. The Gould/Higgie publication photographed coins then in the Mariano Gonzalez collection. The matter is unclear; perhaps Jaime Gonzalez bought Prann's examples, which were then inherited by Mariano Gonzalez. Or perhaps there were three examples of each coin. In 1964, Edward H. Roehrs exhibited his collection, which included an 1877 Morgan dollar with the fleur-de-lis countermark, *Historia Monetaria de Puerto Rico* (Puerto Rico, [1964]), p. 9, no. 5j. The ANS has an example of a fleur-de-lis countermark on an 1880 Morgan dollar from the Philadelphia mint (1985.51.89) but the countermark is clearly a modern fake.

[24] Gregory G. Brunk, *Merchant Countermarks on World Coins* (Rockford, IL, [1989]), pp. 16, 79, 97, 134 (Brunk.52420, 53070, 54680).

[25] *Seaby's Coin and Medal Bulletin* 577 (1966), front cover and p. 302, no. 4003B; *Annual Report of the American Numismatic Society for the Period Ending September 30, 1967* (New York, 1968), p. 10 and pl. 2, 6; Stark (above, n. 19), p. 32.

[26] Harrington E. Manville, "Problems of British Tradesmen's Countermarks on Spanish Dollars," *Actes du 8ème Congrès International de Numismatique* (Paris/Basel, 1976), p. 597.

[27] Brunk (above, n. 24), p. 79.

[28] F. Pridmore, *The Coins of the British Commonwealth of Nations to the End of the Reign of George VI 1952*, Part 3: *Bermuda, British Guiana, British Honduras and the British West Indies* (London, 1965), p. 235, Guadeloupe.10. Pridmore was of the opinion that the countermark was a modern fake, and he is almost certainly right.

[29] Eric P. Newman and Kenneth E. Bressett, *The Fantastic 1804 Dollar* (Racine, WI, 1962), pp. 20-23; Willem (above, n. 2), pp. 10-12.

[30] Richard Giedroyc, "Overstruck 1799 U.S. Silver $1 Survives War in Uruguay: 1844 Siege Peso Struck During War," *Coin World*, September 20, 1993; Richard Giedroyc, "ANS Collection has Overstruck 1798 U.S. Silver $1 from Uruguay," *Coin World*, November 15, 1993.

[31] This is the same specimen which was auctioned by Kagin's (San Diego), Aug. 16-20, 1983 (ANA), 1722. The edge is a leaf edge; the lettered edge undertype is visible reading ONE DOLLAR OR UNIT HUNDRED CENTS.

[32] Ernesto O. Araujo Vilagran, "El 'Peso del Sitio'," *Revista del Instituto Uruguayo de Numismatica* 1956, pp. 19-35; Alcedo F. Almanzar and Dale Seppa, *The Coins of Uruguay, 1840-1971* (San Antonio, 1971), pp. 38-39; Marcos Silvera Antunez, *La Historia de la Patria a Traves de las Monedas*, vol. 1 (Montevideo, 1990), pp. 65-67. Silvera lists the other undertypes as a Spanish 8 reales of 1813, Madrid mint; a Bolivian 8 reales of 1837; and a patagon from the Kingdom of the Two Sicilies.

[33] M. Kenny and C. Gallagher, "The Wellington Bridge Hoard," Colm Gallagher, ed., *Small Change. Papers on Post Medieval Irish Numismatics in Memory of Michael Dolley M.R.I.A.* (Dublin, 1988), pp. 49-52.

[34] S.J. Wilson, "A Preliminary Report on Coins of the Ningaloo or Point Cloates, Wreck Western Australia," *The Australian Coin Review*, October 1979, pp. 3-5; Graeme Henderson, "Indiamen Traders of the East," *Archaeology* 33, 6 (Nov./Dec. 1980), pp. 18-25; Christopher Batio, "Treasures Surface in Shipwreck Salvage," *World Coin News*, March 1, 1993. I have not come across a full listing of the coins in the ANS library.

[35] Philip W. Whitely, "Coin Find Reveals Pioneer Money Usages," *The Numismatist* 1963, pp. 641-42.

[36] Willem (above, n. 2), pp. 48-51.

[37] Another Chinese name for the Carolus dollar was "Fan-mien" (foreign face). The pillar dollar was also called "two candlestick dollars." The U.S. trade dollar was called "precious goose," "precious duck," and "flying hen." The Mexican cap and rays dollar was a "sun dollar." Willem (above, n. 2), pp. 40-41 and 102, n. 1. The Arabs had similarly colorful names for Spanish pillar dollars: "Father of the Pillars" and "Father of the cannons," because the pillars look like cannons if you turn the dollar sideways. The thaler of Empress Mary Theresa, widely used in Arabia and Africa, was called "Father of the eagle" by the Arabs. *Vom Taler zum Dollar* (above, n. 4), p. 187; Charles Morawitz, *Les Finances de la Turquie* (Paris, 1902), p. 283. These

names are interesting in recording how the silver dollars appeared to non-western eyes.

38   Willem (above, n. 2). See also Q. David Bowers, *Silver Dollars and Trade Dollars of the United States* (Wolfeboro, 1993), pp. 869-1086, which includes a chapter by Robert W. Julian based on archival research.

39   de Jesus (above, n. 20), pp. 354-56.

40   A full set with chopmarks was offered when Willem's collection was auctioned after his death. See Henry Christensen, Inc., Sept. 5, 1980, 694-757; Walter Breen, *Walter Breen's Complete Encyclopedia of U. S. and Colonial Coins* (New York, 1988), p. 466 says that a complete set with chopmarks was exhibited at the 1985 ANA convention. The exhibit does not appear to be mentioned in *The Numismatist* because it did not win an award, oddly enough. James Vernon Epps has ranked the chopmarked trade dollars in order of increasing rarity; his list goes 1877-S (commonest), 1878-S, 1874-S, 1874-CC, 1874, 1875-S Type I, 1876-S Type II, 1873-S, 1875-S Type II, 1876-S Type I, 1876-CC Type II, 1875-CC Type I, 1877, 1877-CC, 1876 Type II, 1876 Type I, 1876-CC Type I, 1875 Type I, 1875 Type II, 1873-CC, 1873, 1875 S/CC Type I, 1875-CC Type II and 1878-CC (rarest). Epps, "Our Most Misunderstood Coin - The U.S. Trade Dollar," *The Gobrecht Journal* 4 (Mar. 1978), pp. 13-18.

41   Willem (above, n. 2), p. 148; Bowers (above, n. 38), pp. 900-903 gives dealers' accounts about some hoards they handled. Unfortunately, we lack detailed enumeration of the contents of these hoards, their find spots, their dates of deposit, what other coins (such as Mexican dollars), if any, were in the hoards, and the pots which contained the hoard. A listing of the find spots would be useful to see how far the U.S. trade dollar did penetrate into China.

42   Karl Helfferich, *Georg von Siemens. Ein Lebensbild aus Deutschlands grosser Zeit* (Berlin, 1921) vol. 1, pp. 266-68; Fritz Seidenzahl, *100 Jahre Deutsche Bank 1870-1970* (Frankfurt am Main, [1970]), pp. 36-37; Karl Erich Born, *Geld und Banken im 19. und 20. Jahrhundert* (Stuttgart, 1977), p. 13.

43   Willem (above, n. 2), pp. 103-13.

44   Willem (above, n. 2), pp. 126-36.

45   Willem (above, n. 2), p. 176.

46   "In Folge von Anhäufung von Truppen ist die Nachfrage nach Silberdollars sehr gross geworden und daher der Kurs um 10% gestiegen. Die englischen Banken haben die Gelegenheit benützt um den englischen Dollar einzuführen, der bisher hier zurückgewiesen würde. Die Hongkong + Shanghai Banking Corporation soll für 4 Millionen solcher Dollar nach China gebracht haben, auch die Deutsch-Asiatische Bank hat die bei ihr von den deutschen Truppen bestellten Summen zum Theil in englischen Dollars geliefert." Dr. Knappe, Imperial German Consul in China, Shanghai, 3 October 1900 to the German Foreign Office (arrived Berlin 7 November 1900) in: "Acten betreffend: Aufstand in China; Einschreiten der Mächte vom 6. November 1900 bis 7. November 1900," Politisches Archiv des Auswärtigen Amtes, Bonn, China No. 24, Band 71 (= Az. R 18348).

[47]   Willem (above, n. 2), p. 176.

[48]   "200,000,000 Silver Dollars to be Melted," *The Numismatist* 1918, p. 184; "Now It's 'Dollars by the Bushel'," *The Numismatist* 1919, pp. 118-19; "Trainloads of Silver Cross the Continent," *The Numismatist* 1919, p. 252.

[49]   "China Buys Silver Dollars," *The Numismatist* 1920, p. 13; "The Silver Mystery of China," *The Numismatist* 1920, pp. 165-66.

[50]   Rose (above, n. 22), pp. 25-26.

[51]   Frank H.H. King with David J.S. King and Catherine E. King, *The History of the Hongkong and Shanghai Banking Corporation*, vol. 2, *The Hongkong Bank in the Period of Imperialism and War, 1895- 1918. Wayfoong, the Focus of Wealth* (Cambridge, [1988]), p. 216.

[52]   The gold exchange standard was adopted for India as the result of the conclusions of the Herschell Committee. See *Report of the Committee Appointed to Inquire into the Indian Currency. Presented to Both Houses of Parliament by Command of Her Majesty* (London, 1893), C.7060; John Maynard Keynes, *Indian Currency and Finance* (London, 1913), pp. 33-36.

[53]   "Gold Peso to Be the Unit of Value in the Philippines," *AJN* 40 (1905), p. 17; King (above, n. 50), pp. 216-26; Compton MacKenzie, *Realms of Silver: One Hundred Years of Banking in the East* (London, 1954), pp. 192-93.

[54]   Alberto F. Pradeau, *Numismatic History of Mexico from the Pre-Columbian Epoch to 1823* (Los Angeles, 1938), p. 68.

Appendix 1:
A Restated Opinion on the Origin of the 1804 Dollar and the 1804 Eagle Proofs

Eric P. Newman

**Coinage of the Americas Conference
at the American Numismatic Society, New York**

October 30, 1993

Another updated explanation of the situation giving rise to the U.S. Mint creation of the proof dollar dated 1804, the proof Eagle dated 1804 and related coinage may be surplusage. Nevertheless at this time newly refined and hopefully clarified conclusions may be welcome. It is assumed that the reader has already studied the matter, including reading *The Fantastic 1804 Dollar* published in 1962 and much of the continuing commentary on the subject since then.[1]

A (enlarged). Silver 50 cents showing device designs in current use in 1834 for it and lower denominations, having a capped bust design facing left on the obverse and only 3 arrows in the eagle's claw on the reverse.

1. On November 11, 1834, President Jackson directed that a complete set of the coins of the United States be prepared by the U.S. Mint for presentation to certain foreign rulers and specified "each kind now in use." Another order for additional dignitaries soon followed. For presentation purposes proof coins were deemed desirable.

2. It was thought by the Mint officials that to make a better impression on the foreign dignitaries the largest coins which the U.S. had minted should be included in the sets, even though the largest coins (the silver dollar and the gold Eagle) had not been minted for about 30 years and were not "in use" (in circulation) in 1834. To locate choice examples of previously issued early dollars and Eagles was apparently not considered satisfactory or practical for the purpose.

B (enlarged). Gold 1834 $5 showing device designs in use before June 24, 1834, on gold coinage, with obverse having a capped bust design facing left and reverse having the design of an eagle below a motto and holding 3 arrows.

C (enlarged). Gold 1834 $5 showing device designs in use after June 24, 1834, on gold coinage, with obverse having a classic bust design facing left and reverse having the eagle design without motto and holding 3 arrows.

3. There was a major problem in late 1834 if the Mint determined to include a silver dollar and a gold Eagle in each presentation set. The punches and dies for lower silver and gold denominations for the year 1834 had been prepared earlier in the year and before the presentation set matter arose (see figs. A, B, and C). Since no silver dollars or gold Eagles had been minted for 30 years no new device punches or dies had been prepared for those denominations during that long interval. A substantial amount of work and time would be required for the Mint to engrave new obverse and new reverse device punches for both a silver dollar and a gold Eagle to match current designs on the lower denomination coinage. Dies could be made more quickly and with less work than device punches, but device punches had to be available for dies to be made. Since device punches over 30 years old with obsolete designs happened to be available in 1834, the thought arose that the preparation of new device punches with properly matching designs might be avoided in preparing dies for the silver dollars and gold Eagles for presentation sets, as many of the obsolete ornament, letter and numeral punches had also been retained. The use of the available obsolete device punches to make dies for silver dollars and gold Eagles would save extensive work and time but would result in those coins not matching the designs on the current 1834 coins prepared for the presentation sets. A problem was what date might be cut into those dies. If those two denominations were to be prepared with obsolete designs and dated 1834 a major criticism from American officials and others would obviously have been justified for the creation of previously non-existent coins which did not match the current designs. Was there a proper way to save the work and time to make new device punches and to create a silver dollar as the largest silver coin and the Eagle as the largest gold coin for the few presentation sets needed?

4. The officially published annual U.S. Mint Reports for 1804 and 1805 stated that dollars were "made" by the Mint in the years 1804 and 1805. The handwritten detailed records indicate that these pieces consisted of Spanish-American dollars of various dates and U.S. dollars dated earlier than the year 1804. No U.S. dollar coinage of any kind occurred in 1805. The coinage of silver dollars was banned by order of President Jefferson on May 1, 1806.

5. Because of such officially published statistics, some Mint officials in 1834 had reason to believe that U.S. dollars dated 1804 might have been minted in 1804 and 1805, but found none in the Eckfeldt

D (enlarged). Gold Eagle dated 1804 struck in 1804 with dies prepared in 1804 from punches then in current usage. Obverse design with a capped bust facing right and reverse design with an heraldic eagle holding 13 arrows. Date with crosslet on 4. No Eagles coined after 1804 until diplomatic problem in 1834.

collection at the Mint. Such a belief, although erroneous, was apparently still held in 1842 when Eckfeldt and Du Bois published *A Manual of Gold and Silver Coins* and illustrated the type of U.S. dollar for the "1797-1805" period as having an 1804 date.[2] That period was obviously derived from the officially published Mint Reports rather than the handwritten detailed records. The authors knew however that their book illustration was of an 1804 dollar coined by the U.S. Mint in 1834 from dies cut in 1834. The use of the illustration was an effort to help justify and cover up what the Mint had done in 1834.

6. The officially published annual U. S. Mint Reports for 1804 and 1805 accurately stated that gold Eagles were "made" by the Mint in 1804 and none in 1805 (fig. D). The Eckfeldt collection had retained an example of an Eagle dated 1804 since its coinage in 1804. Feeling they needed proof coins for presentation, the Mint determined to use available obsolete punches to make a pair of new dies in 1834 for an Eagle dated 1804 and strike coins with them.

7. All denominations of U.S. gold and silver coins minted prior to 1828 had a circle of dentils around the border of both obverse and reverse extending radially to the circumferential edge. In 1828 the border design of dimes was modified to a circle of beading within and touching a thin flat raised band along the circumference. This same change of design was applied to half dimes in 1829 and to reduced diameter quarters in 1831. The modified border first appeared on production coinage of half dollars late in 1836, but is also found on both faces of experimental proof half dollars dated 1833, 1834 and 1835 (see above, fig. A). The modified border design is found on the dollars dated 1804 and on the proof dollars dated 1801, 1802 and 1803 which are die-linked through the reverse die to the Class I dollars dated 1804. The modified border design was adopted for production coinage for each denomination to coordinate with the further development of a one-piece collar die (the close or closed collar) to use in striking those coins. A one-piece collar die for dollars was not available for use in production coinage until steam powered presses were introduced at the U.S. Mint in 1836 for Gobrecht dollars which also have the modified border.

8. The Class I dollars dated 1804 were individually struck during 1834 for presentation sets on the U.S. Mint's available medal press using a smooth collar die from which the coin was not extracted automatically (fig. E). During striking the smooth collar crushed the

E. Silver dollar dated 1804 struck in 1834 from dies prepared in late 1834 from retained obsolete punches with device designs having a draped bust facing right with uncovered hair on the obverse and an heraldic eagle holding 13 arrows on the reverse. No dollars had been coined for 30 years prior thereto.

edge lettering which had been put on the planchet by the available Castaing machine and old edge lettering dies. Class II and Class III dollars dated 1804 and the proof dollars dated 1801, 1802 and 1803 were not prepared in 1834 and were struck many years later.

9. The May 1, 1806 presidential ban on coinage of U.S. dollars was officially terminated on April 18, 1831, because of the stabilization of the silver to gold value ratio, but no silver dollar coinage, no silver dollar pattern and no silver dollar device punch resulted and none were then planned. Franklin Peale went to Europe in 1833 to study new minting techniques.

10. If either new device punches or new dies cut with such new punches had been prepared for dollar production in 1831 they would have borne capped bust designs facing left similar to those on the then current subsidiary silver coinage or entirely new designs, rather than a retrogression to the long abandoned draped bust facing right design and the heraldic eagle design used for dollars and other subsidiary silver coins during the period just prior to 1804.

11. Even though there was no specific restriction against coinage of the dollar and Eagle denominations in 1834 it might have been contrary to authority or protocol (as well as the November 11, 1834 instructions) to coin denominations not currently minted.

12. The Mint officials were constantly aware that under the law coins were to be dated with the year in which they were struck. In attempted compliance with that rule in the past the Mint had created

ugly overdating, but there were often minor technical violations of
the law when carryover dies from the preceding year (occasionally
two or three years) were used because they were still in satisfactory condition and it was economically sound to use them until they
wore out or broke. The minting in 1834 of a coin dated 1804 from
newly prepared dies was clearly contrary to law and not within the
foregoing accepted conservation practice.

13. The idea of antedating the dies for the dollar and the Eagle to
a year in which the Mint officials speculated or knew such coinage
had been minted was selected as a way of handling the diplomatic
gift matter with only a modest amount of impropriety or illegality.

14. Mint officials believed that no one (particularly foreign rulers)
would know the difference between a dollar made in 1834 but dated
1804 and a dollar coined in and dated 1804, but if that fact was
learned it was believed that no one would be concerned. This thinking would also have applied to any dollars dated prior to 1804 which
might be minted in 1834 with newly prepared dies.

15. Mint officials therefore considered the possibility of using such
dates as 1801, 1802 or 1803 for dollars to be coined in 1834 for
the presentation sets as they positively knew that there were coins
of such dates in the Eckfeldt collection but were not certain whether
there was or was not a dollar coined in 1804 with an 1804 date.

16. Mint officials also believed that no one (particularly foreign
rulers) would know the difference between an Eagle made in 1834
but dated 1804 and an Eagle coined in 1804 and dated 1804, but
if that fact was learned it was believed that no one would be concerned. Similarly if an Eagle dated 1804 coined in late 1834 contained the larger gold content effective in 1804 rather than the reduced standard effective under the June 28, 1834 Act, this would be
helpful to the deception. Available obsolete device and other punches were used in 1834 to create Eagle dies with the obverse die
dated 1804 and that pair of dies was used to strike Eagles with the
gold content effective in 1804 rather than the gold content required
in late 1834. The Eagle obverse die which was cut in 1834 had no
crosslet on the 4 of the date and otherwise differed slightly from
the Eagle obverse die used in 1804 for striking Eagles dated 1804,
all of which had a crosslet on the 4 of the date. The new heraldic
eagle reverse die used for the $10 Eagle struck in 1834 differs from
all other known heraldic eagle reverse dies of $10 Eagles of any date

and also from all other heraldic eagle reverse dies used at any time for silver half dollars (the heraldic eagle reverse dies on these silver half dollars being the same size and style as those dies used for the gold Eagles). The border beading on the obverse and reverse dies of the Eagles dated 1804 and struck in 1834 differed from the dentils on the borders of the Eagles dated 1804 and struck in 1804. The raised reeds on the edge of the Eagles struck in 1834 were narrower and greater in number than the raised reeds on the edge of the Eagles struck in 1804. Thus the making and use of new dies in late 1834 to strike Eagles dated 1804 with an improper weight and an improper date created Eagle novodels and illegal Eagles (fig. F).

17. In view of the uncertainty of Mint officials in 1834 as to whether dollars dated 1804 had or had not been struck in 1804 and to avoid possible criticism on that account it seemed practical to have alternate dates to choose from and obverse dies dated 1801, 1802 and 1803 were made up at the same time as the new obverse die dated 1804 was cut. When cutting these four obverse dollar dies with the old bust punch (probably brittle from prior use) a curl on the top of the head of that device punch broke off after it was used on the first two pieces of die stock. This went unnoticed. In preparing the four obverse dies the four selected dates were punched in randomly. Each die thus had an equal chance of having either a complete curl or a broken curl. It so happened that the die dated 1804 had a broken curl as did the die dated 1801. The dies dated 1802 and 1803 each had an unbroken curl.

18. Because four differently dated obverse dies happened to be prepared for coining the dollar for the presentation sets there were several obverse dies available for substitution in case of obverse die breakage. Only two reverse dies were prepared because either could be paired with any obverse die and one spare reverse die was adequate for possible substitution. This situation might explain why more obverse dies than reverse dies were prepared which was not a customary practice for production coinage.

19. The fact that in 1834 the star punches used on the obverse dollar die dated 1801 and the figure punches for that die were of a different style than those used at the same time for obverse dollar dies dated 1802, 1803 and 1804 was coincidental as sets of various sizes of all these styles of punches were available in 1834 at the Mint because of prior use of those styles on other denominations of U.S. Mint coinage.

F (enlarged). Gold Eagle dated 1804 struck in 1834 with dies prepared in late 1834 from retained obsolete device punches. Obverse design with a capped bust facing right and reverse design with an heraldic eagle holding 13 arrows. Date with no crosslet on 4.

20. It was deemed that only one new pair of dies was needed for the Eagle dated 1804 because striking a few gold coin examples in the medal press would not result in die breakage, particularly because gold was softer than silver and the Eagle was thin. Because it was then known that Eagles dated 1804 had been coined in 1804 no other substitute dates were needed for making Eagles for the presentation sets.

21. The obverse dollar die dated 1804 and the reverse die (designated variety X) were selected for use in minting the dollars for the diplomatic coin sets and the extra examples. The Mint officials in 1834 therefore created an unknown dollar dated 1804 hoping or thinking that they had reproduced a previously existing coin. The dollar dated 1804 thus created was a novodel dollar and an illegal dollar.

22. The remaining 1801, 1802 and 1803 obverse dollar dies and the remaining reverse die (designated variety Y) were not needed or used for the preparation of the diplomatic coin sets and were (along with the dies which were used for that diplomatic purpose) available for devilment and connivance thereafter. From these dies novodel dollars dated 1801, 1802 and 1803 were made in later years as well as dollars dated 1804 known as Class II and Class III 1804 dollars. The word "restrike" is improperly applied to the novodel dollars dated 1801, 1802 and 1803 as there are no known prior strikes using any of their obverse dies. Their reverse die however had been used in 1834 for the Class I 1804 novodel dollars.

23. In the exchange with Matthew A. Stickney on May 9, 1843, the Mint traded a dollar dated 1804 for a 1785 Immune Columbia gold piece. Both parties received coins not struck at the time of their dating and each probably thought he was fooling the other.

24. The affidavits and letters of Mint officials inferring or stating that the dollars dated 1804 were coined in 1804 were a deliberate attempt to cover up their mistakes and improper acts undertaken at the Mint in 1834 or early 1835 when the coins dated 1804 for the presentation sets were being prepared.

25. The experimental proof half dollars dated 1833, 1834 and 1835 (previously referred to in section 7), in addition to having beading inside a raised thin flat border band on both faces: (I) have planchets which were edge lettered before striking; (II) have edge let-

tering which was crushed when struck in the U.S. Mint medal press; and (III) have the identical reverse die which was used in 1836 for edge lettered half dollar production coinage in combination with a new obverse die dated 1836 having dentils extending radially to the circumference, such combination being known as Overton variety 106.[3] Whether the 1833, 1834 and 1835 experimental proof half dollars were struck during the year of their dating or at some time prior to the transfer in 1836 of the reverse die to production coinage (when reverse die breaks occurred) does not seem certain. Thus the dies made for and the striking of such experimental proof half dollars may have taken place during late 1834 and thereafter. The above described 1836 half dollar variety appears to be the only United States coin which has a border with dentils extending radially to the circumference on one face and beading inside a raised thin flat border band on the other face.

Virtually all of the foregoing is based upon presently undisputed facts. Some is based upon what the writer considers ordinary and obvious human attitudes and thinking. Each reader is naturally free to retain, develop or change his own opinion on any of the foregoing points wherever new specific historical or scientific data may arise or the thoughts expressed herein do not meet with the reader's satisfaction.

For over 33 years Kenneth E. Bressett and I have continually shared our findings and thoughts on this intriguing subject and he has contributed to the foregoing position paper and agrees with it. The cooperation of the American Numismatic Society, the Harry W. Bass, Jr. Research Foundation, Q. David Bowers and Thomas Serfass is also much appreciated.

[1] Eric P. Newman and Kenneth E. Bressett, *The Fantastic 1804 Dollar* (Racine, WI, 1962). A recent summary of the literature appears in Eric P. Newman and Kenneth E. Bressett, "*The Fantastic 1804 Dollar*: 25th Anniversary Follow-up," *America's Silver Coinage, 1794-1891*, COAC Proceedings 3 (New York, 1987), pp. 153-75.

[2] Jacob R. Eckfeldt and William E. Du Bois, *A Manual of Gold and Silver Coins* (Philadelphia, 1842)

[3] A.C. Overton, *Early Half Dollar Die Varieties, 1794-1836* (Colorado Springs, CO, 1967).

Appendix 2:
A Pair of Morgan Dollar Dies in the Collection of the American Numismatic Society

John M. Kleeberg

Coinage of the Americas Conference
at the American Numismatic Society, New York

October 30, 1993

In the course of looking for suitable items for exhibit in connection with the Coinage of the Americas Conference on the United States silver dollar, I found a pair of dies for the 1883-CC Morgan dollar among the collection (figs. 1-2).

Old dies from the United States Mint have been in the hands of collectors since the very beginnings of interest in United States coinage; one of the earliest American coin collectors, Joseph J.

1

2

Mickley, came into possession of various old dies and seems to have been behind the production of a number of restrikes using them, notably the 1804, 1810, and 1823 cents. None of the dies used for those cent restrikes are now in the ANS collection, but the ANS does have the obverse die for an 1818 large cent. Although used dies have been part of the collecting scene since the 1850s, if not before, they have been relatively little studied and catalogued, at least compared with the attention that has been given to the coins. For example, Walter Breen mentions in his encyclopedia that restrikes have been made using the die of the 1805 quarter (Browning 2),[1] but he did not mention that the die has ended up in the collection of the ANS (1923.33.2, gift of M. Knoedler, probably from the Ellsworth estate).

The two Morgan dollar dies in the ANS collection have the numbers 1940.53.1-2; they are the gift of T. James Clarke in 1940. The dies have been cancelled by putting a large X-shaped gash in them. They are significantly larger than the dies the ANS has from the early nineteenth century, indicating the progress of minting technology, which moves toward larger and heavier dies.

The Carson City Mint numbered its dies. On the side of the die with the head of liberty is the mark "No 17"; on the side of the die with the eagle is the mark "No. 14/1883."[2] A date was not necessary on the head die because the head has the date below it. The mark of the date on the eagle die indicates that the Mint regarded the dies of one particular year as a discreet group by this time, and would not mix the reverse die of an earlier year with the obverse of a later one; thus if the Mint was doing its work properly, students of the die combinations of the Morgan dollar series should not come across any "biennial dies." It is interesting to note that the study of Morgan dollar die varieties by Van Allen and Mallis lists only seven different head dies and four eagle dies for the date and mintmark combination 1883-CC, so there are presumably many more to discover, judging by the numbers on the side of the steel dies in the ANS collection.[3]

The United States Mint did report the number of dies used to produce the coins in each year; but since the Mint, like the rest of the government, was on a fiscal year of July 1-June 30, the figures do not give us the true number of dies used in a calendar year. For July 1, 1882 to June 30, 1883, the Mint at Philadelphia made 20 dies for Carson City; and for July 1, 1883 to June 30, 1884, the Mint made another 20 dies for Carson City. The figures in the reports must refer to dies, not die pairs, because the Mint was in the habit of using the same reverse die for the annual assay medal through the four years of a presidential administration, and it is only when the administration changes that the number of dies reported as made for the annual assay medal jumps from one to two. We can therefore deduce that the figures in the mint reports refer to individual dies, rather than die pairs. One might then assume that 20 dies were made for Carson City in the calendar year 1883. Q. David Bowers, in his 1993 work on silver dollars of the United States, gives the figure of 10 obverse dies and 10 reverse dies for Carson City; Bowers does not indicate whether this figure comes from the mint reports or from archival documents, but it might have been based on archival research by R. W. Julian.[5] This figure is, however, contradicted by the evidence of our dies: they suggest that Carson City received at least 31 dies (14 plus 17). In my opinion the figures in the mint reports are not to be trusted, and are just approximations. The Carson City die figures in general tend to be round numbers, which suggest that some clerk prepared rough estimates for the annual audit. The evidence of the dies also contradicts the evidence which apparently comes from archival research in the Mint, but the document in the archives may be similar rough figures prepared by the same clerk. This reinforces the significance of our dies, the evidence of which contradicts the evidence of the annual reports.

The eagle die has a notch, which the liberty head die does not; this suggests that the eagle die was the fixed, lower die, and the liberty head die the upper, moveable one, which is confirmed by the studies of Van Allen and Mallis.[6] In classical numismatics, the obverse is considered to be the lower die, because the lower die is fixed and breaks less than the upper die, and therefore the more complicated type is put on the lower die. This is also true of the Morgan dollar: the eagle side is the more complicated type, and is therefore the side a mint would want to be the fixed, lower die. One question we have not been able to solve is if the Philadelphia Mint prepared and sent out different numbers of head (strictly speaking, reverse) and eagle (strictly speaking, obverse) dies. The Mint should send out more head dies, because that die would break more frequently. The ANS dies suggest that would be the case: the head is die number 17, the eagle die number 14.

In short, this pair of Morgan dollar dies indicates that the study of the actual dies themselves should be a fruitful area for further numismatic research, because their evidence often contradicts evidence from normal die studies and printed sources.

[1]   Walter Breen, *Walter Breen's Complete Encyclopedia of U.S. and Colonial Coins* (New York, 1988), p. 338.

[2]   I am using the expression "head die" and "eagle die" instead of obverse and reverse. Although common usage calls the head the obverse, and the eagle the reverse, on two definitions: the side struck by the lower die, and the side with the title and emblems of the issuing authority, the eagle side is the obverse, and the head side the reverse.

[3]   Leroy C. Van Allen and A. George Mallis, *Comprehensive Catalog and Encyclopedia of Morgan and Peace Dollars* (Virginia Beach, 1991), p. 251.

[4]   United States. Bureau of the Mint. *Annual Report of the Director of the Mint to the Secretary of the Treasury for the Fiscal Year Ended June 30, 1883* (Washington, 1883), pp. 6, 44; United States. Bureau of the Mint. *Annual Report of the Director of the Mint to the Secretary of the Treasury for the Fiscal Year Ended June 30, 1884* (Washington, 1884), pp. 6, 44.

[5]   Q. David Bowers, *Silver Dollars & Trade Dollars of the United States. A Complete Encyclopedia.* (Wolfeboro, NH, 1993), vol. 2, p. 2353. (Note: not paginated consecutively. Volume 1 ends on p. 1096; volume 2 begins on p. [1997]). Cf. vol 1, p. xi: Julian "provided mintage figures, die production figures, and other data from Mint records."

[6]   Van Allen and Mallis (above, n. 3), p. 59.